The Nursing Home Experience

THE NURSING HOME EXPERIENCE

A Family Guide to Making It Better

Marylou Hughes

Crossroad | *New York*

1992

The Crossroad Publishing Company
370 Lexington Avenue, New York, NY 10017

Copyright © 1992 by Marylou Hughes

All rights reserved. No part of this book may be reproduced, stored in a retrieval system, or transmitted, in any form or by any means, electronic, mechanical, photocopying, recording, or otherwise without the written permission of The Crossroad Publishing Company.

Printed in the United States of America

Library of Congress Cataloging-in-Publication Data

Hughes, Marylou.
 The nursing home experience : a family guide to making it better / Marylou Hughes.
   p.   cm.
 ISBN 0-8245-1190-5
  1. Nursing home care. 2. Nursing home patients—Family relationships. 3. Consumer education. I. Title.
RA997.H83   1992
362.1'6—dc20   91-39781
                                                          CIP

To Inta and Gus Sraders

Contents

Introduction	11
Author's Note	13
1 Arrangements and Adjustments: Making the Decision	**15**
When to Place	16
Never Say Never	16
Caregiver's Health	17
Patient's Health	18
People in the Middle	19
Setting Priorities	19
Being a Prisoner	20
Personality Conflicts	21
Do Not Want to Be a Burden	22
Family Differences	23
What the Nursing Home Offers	24
Burnout	25
Where to Place	26
Location	27
Look	27
Feel	30
Facts	31
Charges	31
Medical Care	34
Staffing	35
Physician Visits	36
A Living Will	37
Final Arrangements	37
Technology	38
Family Notification	38

8 | Contents

Restoration	39
Room Change Policies	39
Miscellaneous	40
Concerns	40
Preferences	41
Making the Adjustment	43
Coping with Stress	44
Medical Attention	46
Social Supports	47
Play a Part in Planning	48
Honesty	49
Timely and Usable Information	49
Assistance	50
Adjustment Reactions	51
Regression	51
Denial	52
Hostility	52
Immobility	53
Anxiety	54
Physical Symptoms	55
Family Adjustment	56
Recognize Your Feelings	56
Accept Your Feelings	57
Work through, around, and with Your Feelings	58

2 Residents' Rights — **60**

Choice	61
Responsibility	62
Self-Respect	65
Dignity and Respect	67
No Harsh or Abusive Treatment	67
Freedom to Meet	70
Resident Council	71
Family Council	72
Freedom of Speech	72
Quality of Life	74
Residents' Rights Dilemmas	74

3 Life after Placement — **78**

Stay Involved	78
Importance of Family	79
Advocacy	79
Support	80

Contents | 9

Restorative	80
See the Benefits	81
The Resident's New Life	81
Game Playing	83
Education on Aging	84
Activities	86
Community Activities	87
Rides	88
Holidays	89
Friends	89
Clubs	90
Interests	90
Learning	90
Entertainment	91
Nursing Home Activities	91
Companions	95

4 Personal Possessions   **99**

Preparing the Place	99
Clothes	100
Helpful Items	102
The Extras	106
Problems with Possessions	108

5 Visiting Techniques   **112**

Visiting Tips	114

6 The Nursing Home Staff   **128**

The Staff's Responsibilities and Viewpoints	128
When to Communicate with the Staff	133
How to Talk with the Staff and Problem-Solve	135

Glossary	145
Worksheet	155

Introduction

Most residents in most nursing homes do not need intensive medical care. Instead, they need assisted living and supervision. This book is geared to that majority. Not that most residents don't have medical problems; they do. But they are up and around and benefit from the social and recreational aspects of the nursing home program. If your relative is bedridden, and you are mainly concerned with nursing care, this book is still for you. You will be helped with your feelings, you will understand what you can expect from nursing home care, and you will learn how to communicate with the nursing home staff.

You may not need to read the entire book, but concentrate on those parts that presently concern you. Keep this book as a reference, and consult the helpful glossary——it will inform and reassure you.

Being a relative of a nursing home resident is a complicated role. There is no right, wrong, or perfect way to manage the situation. You care. You do the best you can. Some days it looks and feels good. Other days it seems that everything is bad. Don't feel you have to do it all. You can't. It is the author's hope that this book will give you the encouragement you need, answer some questions, and help you to realize that you are managing well.

Author's Note

The identities of the people written about in this book have been carefully disguised in accordance with professional standards of confidentiality and in keeping with their rights to privileged communication with the author.

1
Arrangements and Adjustments: Making the Decision

Placing someone you know in a nursing home is one of life's unpleasant and unwanted experiences, and it becomes more inevitable as people live longer, families are dispersed, and more adults now work outside the home. Since 43 percent of the elderly live in nursing homes at some time in their years and 5 percent are in a nursing home at any given time, it is an event that touches many lives. As is the case with a number of life's problems, there is no perfect way to handle it and we have no set formulas that will make everything right. There are, however, steps, attitudes, and procedures that can make placement less difficult and result in more positive adjustments. From the first you must adopt the attitude that you will do the best you can and will accept the fact that you are exerting your best efforts.

Making the decision to place a loved one in a nursing home frequently comes at a time of crisis and is not a matter of planned choice. When this happens there is little time for thoughtful preparation and selection. The nursing home with the available bed is the one that is accepted. Crisis occurs when families can no longer take the stress of providing twenty-four-hour care to the elderly relative or the relative who has a medical emergency that results in hospitalization and nursing home placement.

It is encouraging to see more people taking a realistic view of present-day life and making thought-through decisions for themselves should they no longer be able to manage their own day-to-day care. These people are buying insurance that will pay for long-term care. They are making their intentions known to family, friends, and legal and medical advisors. They are checking out the nursing homes in their communities. If the elderly family members have not made their plans, the relatives will be an integral part of the decision and be faced with the planning and the footwork. It is not an easy job. It is less traumatic and emotionally laden, however, when the relative or person involved knows that he or she is doing the right thing in the best possible way.

WHEN TO PLACE

If the placement has not been forced as a response to a medical emergency the decision may have to be made as the result of family pressures. Nursing home care should be considered an option rather than something to avoid. In many instances it is the best available option.

Never Say Never

A good many families have promised that their husbands, wives, mothers, fathers, will never go to a nursing home. They have this rule imprinted on their minds as a guide for living, as fixed as the knowledge that they should not walk in front of a moving car or throw a ball in a china shop. The promise of never placing a loved one in a nursing home is on the same level: a moving car will hit and hurt the person in front of it or a thrown ball will shatter a glass object on impact. The promise to care for a spouse or parent is made with the thought that time will not dramatically alter circumstances. It does. People go to work. Health deteriorates. Children grow up and need more room and privacy in the household. There are financial stresses. Roles and personalities clash.

Mrs. A vowed that her mother would never live in a nursing home as long as Mrs. A lived. When Mrs. A's father died her mother lived alone. When she became physically fragile she moved into a small apartment near the A's. This put more of a burden on Mrs. A because she checked on her mother daily, cleaned her house, and did her laundry. She took her mother shopping. When the A's children became teenagers Mrs. A went to work to help pay for their more expensive needs and because she felt she had left her own career on hold long enough. She did not reckon with her mother's failing ability to cope. Mother did not eat regularly. Sometimes she forgot to take her pills, or thought she forgot and took them again. The stove was left on, ruining pots and pans. One time a small fire erupted. The toilet ran, the tub overflowed. Her mother wore the same dress all week. She called the police in the night whenever a sound frightened her. Nurses were hired, but Mrs. A's mother fired them. Besides, the expense was more than she could afford. Mrs. A supplemented the cost. This used up her salary. She decided to quit work and take care of her mother in the A family home. Mother was moved. She didn't like it. She was used to living alone and adhering to her own schedule. Her daughter didn't do things to her liking. The teenagers were too noisy, too casual in their dress, and too disrespectful. Mr. A complained that he never got to see his wife alone. They were not one big happy household. It got worse.

Mother got up one night, became confused in the unfamiliar surroundings, tripped over a tennis racket that a teenager had left leaning against the wall, fell, and broke her hip. The hospital staff suggested a nursing home for rehabilitation. Mrs. A remembered her promise never to place her mother in a nursing home and refused to consider it.

Mother was in a hospital bed in the middle of the living room so she could be involved in household life. The children stopped bringing their friends home as she was incontinent and confused. They were embarrassed and did not know how to handle guests. Mrs. A tried to keep everybody happy. No one was. Neither was she. They decided to explore nursing home placement. Mrs. A felt guilty. They all felt relief.

Caregiver's Health

Human beings are capable of ignoring their own needs to take care of loved ones. Caregivers who have health problems themselves end up taking care of a person with a more demanding deterioration. As laudatory as this may be in theory, it is dangerous in practice. The relatives and friends have two people, rather than one person, to worry about. The unhealthy caregivers may not be able to give the unhealthier family members as much care as they need. Under the stress of giving constant care the caregivers' health ebbs to the point of exhaustion, hospitalization, or death. If the care is too much for the caregivers to manage physically, it is wrong for them to do it because they have a responsibility to themselves and because they do not have the strength to give the elderly patients all that is needed.

Mrs. B, diagnosed with Alzheimer's disease, was cared for by her husband. She was seventy, he seventy-nine, with heart problems. The two children, a male pharmacist and a female nurse, lived in another state.

Mr. B took his wife from doctor to doctor until he finally heard that there was nothing that could be done for her. He then decided to devote his life to her care. He told the children nothing other than to assure them that all was going well.

When the B's daughter arrived for a visit she was horrified. Her father was taking nitro for his angina in mega doses. Her mother was unable to recognize her, walk, or feed herself. She was insistent that nursing home placement occur as her father was killing himself and her mother needed more care than any one person could give. Mr. B reluctantly agreed to let his daughter apply for admission to a local nursing home, but he felt that his daughter was betraying her mother. He thought he was, too. After nursing home placement was effected he realized that his wife was receiving from the nursing home staff the care she needed, he was still able to be with her regularly, and his physical health improved.

Patient's Health

What starts out as possible may turn out to be impossible as time goes on. The older couple who were mutually supportive may no longer be so when one more impairment or problem occurs.

Mr. and Mrs. C managed by compensating for each other. She

could not stand so he did the cooking and cleaning. He could not see well so she took care of the bills. Between the two of them they survived quite satisfactorily with assistance from community agencies that provided transportation and shopping services. When Mr. C developed a back problem that kept him from physical activity they had to consider nursing home placement.

People in the Middle

The people caught in the middle are those with young adult children and elderly parents who are in the same area, in the family home, and who need and expect attention. Instead of lessening responsibilities, the demands on their time and energy increase. At the same time health problems may set in. Their own goals are put on hold or go unrecognized. Can the sandwich generation do it all? Should they? Who will look out for them?

Coincident to Mr. D's father moving in with them, their twenty-year-old daughter dropped out of college and settled into her old room. The time the D's planned to use to get to know each other again was taken over with family responsibilities. They did not have time for themselves or each other. Under the stress, Mrs. D's arthritis acted up and Mr. D discovered that he had high blood pressure. Mr. D's father and the D's daughter demanded not hard, but constant, work and schedule adjustments. Aggravations beset everyone. They coped until Mr. D's father started misplacing his belongings and accusing the family members of stealing. Everybody in the household was constantly angry and on edge; it was time to think of other living arrangements.

Setting Priorities

How many years are there for healthy middle-aged people? Time runs out. The spouse torn between the husband/wife and the parent ends up feeling bitter toward both and personally thwarted. It is destructive to try to please everyone because it is impossible. Couples need to make sure that the good years are not gone before they have had any pleasure from them. If a parent needs more than a person can comfortably give without forsaking his or her own life, it is time to set limits.

Mrs. E's mother never could see what her daughter saw in Mr. E. When her daughter moved to be closer to her so she could keep an eye on her, the mother fantasized long hours of companionship between the two of them. Mr. E could entertain himself. Whenever the E's planned a trip, mother became ill. Whenever the E's sat down to eat, mother telephoned. The dependence progressed until mother could not be left alone. As she declined she got more demanding. Mrs. E worked harder. Mr. E got more discouraged. Mrs. E had to see a counselor to get help in setting priorities and finally helping mother make arrangements for nursing home care.

Being a Prisoner

Care of the confused and disoriented requires twenty-four-hour supervision. They lose their way. They get upset for no apparent reason. They are easily threatened and become agitated. They have a distorted sense of time. With their forgetfulness and tendency to wander off they can become dangerous to themselves. Constant vigilance is needed. One person, even two people, cannot keep the ambulatory disoriented person safe even though they sacrifice their own lives to do so. Nursing home staff find it difficult to consistently monitor the residents with these problems, but they are better equipped to do so with around-the-clock staffing, a building outfitted with safety features, and, in many cases, electronic protective measures.

The nursing home setting offers another advantage for disoriented people. There is structure and routine. The confused are easily upset by changes in schedule, unexpected happenings, and too much sensory stimulation. In long-term-care facilities the same kind of people do the same things in the same way every day. The staff can and must adhere to their schedule. What may appear boring offers security, comfort, predictability, and control to those who have very little inner control and lack a sense of personal security. After a period of settling in to new sights, smells, stimuli, and surroundings, the disoriented feel at home and safe in the nursing home setting.

Mrs. F, an elderly woman, lived in a mobile home park with her husband, who had been diagnosed with Alzheimer's disease. She was determined to care for Mr. F at home because change upset him. But she was having trouble dealing with him and with her neighbors. Every evening he suffered sundown symptoms consisting of anxiety, belligerence, and hyperactivity. He became agitated, would escape from the house, wander into neighbors' homes, trample their flower beds, and at one point drove off in someone else's car. He was apprehended by the police after a minor traffic accident. Mrs. F feared the ire of her neighbors and her husband's violent tantrums, and was frantic for his safety. She wanted something done, but resisted nursing home placement. It was only after he left home and was missing for a night that she realized she had to make the move. At first she was upset with the placement as Mr. F seemed more confused and upset. After a period of consistent care he responded to the stability and was clearly content with the nursing home lifestyle. Mrs. F could let go of her guilt, realize she did the right thing, and take care of herself, while providing support and encouragement to her husband. She was no longer a prisoner in her own home.

Personality Conflicts

Daughters and sons, parents and grandparents, may all love each other, but find it impossible to live together. People have their own personalities, priorities, values, beliefs, habits, interests, obligations, and schedules that may not accommodate those of the people they care about. In many instances love is easier if it is not tested by day-to-day contact.

Daughters and mothers who are devoted to each other may have little in common and different lifestyles. Fathers and sons may enjoy each other's company on outings, but disagree on what is important in life and have dissimilar values.

People who can love and have pleasure in each other for years may find these positive thoughts and actions transformed to resentment and despair when they are forced to live together.

Mrs. G found herself talking with a counselor about her father-in-law. She was faced with caring for him, and he expected women to obey his wishes. Her husband avoided the man as he could not bring himself to confront him. He had always admired and loved his father, but was also afraid of him. Mrs. G felt abused and used. She was considering divorce. The counselor had to get the three of them talking and made a home visit to initiate this. She found that all were miserable. The father expected more from Mr. G and took out his resentment on Mrs. G. Most of all, Mr. G's father hated being dependent. They opted for a try at nursing home living so they could be friends again.

Do Not Want to Be a Burden

Most people are terrified of being dependent. Even dependent people, who seem to ask more than anyone can give, do not want to be a burden on someone else, especially their children. If asked, most people will say they do not want to live in a nursing home. But there is a problem: they do not want to impose on their children, do not want institutional care, and cannot care for themselves. Because of this avoidance-avoidance conflict many elderly live alone in unsafe and unsavory environments long past the time that other arrangements should have been made. If parents are asked before they are faced with the necessity of dependency, they can more easily explain their feelings and opt for group living versus having their children responsible for them. The elderly want their families to care about them, not for them.

Mrs. H was alert and oriented and in a wheelchair. She was physically handicapped to the point she could not live alone. Her daughter and son-in-law took her in. Two strong-minded people (the mother and the son-in-law) were incessantly in conflict while the pacifier (the daughter) tried to keep the peace. No one disagreed when Mrs. H said she wanted to go live in a nursing home. In the nursing home she continued to be assertive, but the consequences were not so distressing to her. The staff did not have to take her criticisms personally. She could be friends with her family when they did not have to live together. She avowed that it was her choice to live in the nursing home. She made the facility her home, made friends, and was involved in the Resident Council and many activities. She felt she made a contribution.

Family Differences

It is a fact of life that one family member frequently becomes the self-appointed and unanimously acclaimed caregiver. That does not mean that he or she is crazy about the job. It means that they feel responsible, the responsibility is gladly given them, and they do not see any way to get out of it. At times they may feel virtuous and proud of their abilities and dependability. Other times they feel put upon.

These duty-bound persons are expected to take charge when a near and dear relative needs care. They respond as expected. When it involves a sick and disabled parent or sibling they may have more than they care to manage and no easy way to absolve themselves of the obligation. The relatives have never found it necessary to pitch in before and cannot see themselves doing so now. They may, however, have plenty of advice to offer, such as "Do not place mother in a nursing home," "Father should be in a nursing home," "Get someone to help (not them)," or "The parents cannot afford long-term care." Discontented parents complain about the caregiver to the caregiver's siblings—who respond with criticisms and suggestions. The designated providers end up guilty, resentful, hurt, exasperated, and feeling that they cannot do anything right.

Mrs. I (It is usually the woman in the caregiver role) found her mother unable to function alone. Mrs. I worked outside the home, and had children and a husband who needed her attention. She could not maintain the mother in the mother's home even with daily visits and help with cleaning, cooking, and laundry. None of the four siblings could care for her or come to the area to evaluate and help make arrangements for her. At the same time they did not want mother in a nursing home, did not want mother's funds spent on nursing home care, and let Mrs. I know that they thought she was doing the wrong thing, acting hastily, and being selfish. They had talked to mother, who sounded fine.

Mrs. I had to act in the face of family animosity. Her mother was cooperative with her, but continued to complain to the siblings. Mrs. I knew she did what had to be done, but was bitter about her family's reaction. It was much later, after visits to the area, when they evaluated the circumstances firsthand, that they could admit that Mrs. I had assisted their mother in the right way.

What the Nursing Home Offers

Many elderly people need what the nursing home has to offer. Entering a nursing home does not necessarily signal the end of all that makes life worthwhile. It can make life meaningful again. Those who are isolated, neglecting their persons, and living on the outer limits of safety, nutrition, and cleanliness can benefit from life in long-term care.

Mrs. J looked as though she was going to die. She went from doctor to doctor to get treatment for her various ailments. She kept getting worse. When she no longer was able to get to the bathroom she accepted the need for nursing home placement. There, with constant medical supervision her medications and maladies were sorted out and she prospered and became a contributing resident of the facility.

Mrs. K went to the nursing home because she was homeless and sick. She was diagnosed with cancer, received treatment, and was transferred from the hospital. She was alienated from her family, who were tired of her problems and her lifestyle. She was alcoholic and a manic-depressive. She found that the security of the nursing home, where her physical and mental health were monitored, gave her a new lease on life. She participated in activities, field trips, the Resident Council, and support groups, and served as a volunteer. The staff respected her. She saw herself as vital and her self-esteem improved markedly. She made amends with her grown children and reported she was having the best time of her life.

Mr. L arrived at the nursing home physically sick and mentally disoriented. A regimen of good nutrition, exercise, and a predictable schedule improved his health and cleared his mind. He was able to be discharged to a group living home.

Burnout

A task cheerfully undertaken can become a nightmare when it is onerous and unrewarding and seems to go on forever. Caregivers who want to help may find themselves overextended when increasingly more is required of them. Time and energy are limited. No one has an infinite amount of either. Caregivers should be alert to burnout (Cannot take it anymore!) signs and symptoms. They are as follows:

1. You feel you have no time for yourself.
2. There is no place to go to get away.
3. All your family seems to do is complain.
4. Your health is suffering.
5. You are irritable.
6. You have sleep disturbances and dread getting up in the morning.
7. You overeat, take drugs or alcohol to feel good.
8. You resent the relative for whom you are caring.
9. Your work and social life are totally disrupted by caregiving duties.
10. There is no satisfaction in what you do.
11. You feel you can never do enough.
12. The situation seems hopeless.
13. You feel tired all the time.
14. You feel guilty about your feelings.

It should be apparent that when the situation becomes this onerous, no one is happy. No one can win. It is time to give in to what has to be done. The caregivers' misery is a symptom of the universal discontent of all those involved, and it is the caretakers' responsibility to take care of themselves. There comes a time when the resources of the community must be utilized. If the caregiving is directed toward an elderly relative who continues to go downhill, no matter what the caregivers do, a nursing home may be the plan of choice. If the caretakers do not act, someone else may act for them—and it may not be in the way the caretakers want.

WHERE TO PLACE

The useful plan is to have a nursing home in mind before the necessity of placement. A name on the waiting list is not an obligation to accept admission. The name can be left on, put back on, or taken off the list as circumstances dictate. Urge your elderly relative to think about the future before the future arrives. Even if a nursing home is a choice no one wants to make, making a choice is helpful psychologically. It gives a feeling of some control. There is the sense of being prepared. Choice includes an attitude of considering an alternative. The possibility of living in a nursing home is no longer rejected. It provides people with the knowledge that they are acting wisely and carefully and doing all they can do in an untenable situation. It emphasizes that the choosers are doing something for themselves instead of having something done to them.

Nursing home placement should not be carried out without the primary person being involved. No matter how short the preparation time, it needs to be done with the nursing home applicant. Planning and preparation must include the prospective nursing home resident.

It is hard to know how to bring up the subject of nursing home placement. Be honest and straightforward about it. Do not act as though it is the end of the world. Feed in some positive thought about nursing home placement. Visit a nursing home or someone in a nursing home with your relative. Explain what the nursing home can do for them. Know in your own mind why you cannot be a caregiver and share these reasons with your relative. Even if the reasons are obvious, it will be nice for your relative to know that you have thought about it and reached your decision based on tangible reasons that have nothing to do with rejection and shirking of responsibility. Stay as upbeat as you can.

As you go through the selection process share your observations and feelings with your relative. Include the relative every step of the way. If the relative can be included in the tedious efforts of visiting and interviewing, do so. If he or she cannot be, narrow the possibilities until there are two or three nursing homes to choose from. Then let the relative make the final decision. If there are many to evaluate, it may seem too overwhelming for them to look and decide on all of them. If you have strong feelings about what you want in a nursing home, eliminate the ones that do not meet your standards before presenting the choices.

Location

Location is your first consideration. If you plan to visit frequently you and your loved one need to look at nursing homes easily reached and conveniently located. If you know of a marvelous facility one hundred miles from anyone your relative knows do not bother looking at it unless no one plans to visit anyway. The purpose of location is to find a facility near family members. Visits are so important to nursing home residents that the location that enables visits to be made should be the first element considered. This means that the spouse or parent should be in a nursing home in the same part of town in which the prospective visitors live. If mother has been living in Florida and the relatives live in Minnesota, nursing homes in Minnesota should be explored unless mother insists that she prefers good weather to good visits. And she should be allowed to change her mind about this at any time.

Look

It is hard to define what a nursing home is because it is so many things. It is difficult to know what to look for as there are so many roles the facility must fulfill.

A nursing home is a medical facility staffed by members of the medical community such as doctors, nurses, and nursing assistants. But it is not a hospital.

A nursing home provides activities and entertainment for everyone who lives there. It employs activity coordinators, recreation specialists, and music and art therapists. But it is not a recreation center.

A nursing home offers rehabilitation and has physical, occupational, and speech therapists on its staff. But it is not a rehabilitation center.

A nursing home serves regular meals, posts a menu, and on occasion has special dinners and parties with food as an important item. It has on its payroll dietitians and cooks, but it is not a restaurant.

A nursing home employs social workers and psychiatrists who diagnose, treat, and offer counseling and support. But it is not a mental health clinic.

A nursing home dispenses medicines and is regularly checked by a pharmacist, but it is not a drug store.

A nursing home provides laundry services, a hair salon, room cleaning, room service, and other amenities, but it is not a hotel.

A nursing home has a whirlpool, provides monitoring of weight and health status, determines a proper diet and watches what is eaten, encourages exercises, and helps the residents be the best that they can be. But it is not a spa.

All these components make up the whole that is the long-term-care facility. Each of these parts is required for the nursing home to be approved and licensed.

When you look at the facility look at each aspect of the nursing home program, with emphasis on the part that is the most important to you and your relative.

Is the landscaping neat and attractive? Are the hallways clean and free of clutter? Do the furnishings look as though they have seen better days or are they crisp, comfortable, inviting? Pay attention to your first impressions. Does the facility look good? Do you get the message that the staff cares about their facility and are interested in making a good first and lasting impression?

Are there many call lights on over the residents' rooms? If not, this means that the nursing staff is anticipating the residents' needs and taking care of them before they have to call for help. If lights are on, are they switched off quickly by nurses and assistants answering the residents' calls promptly? Is the facility free of excretory odors? This shows that the nursing staff is keeping the residents clean, giving them fast and appropriate attention, and that the housekeeping department is giving good backup in the team effort to respond to the residents' medical and personal-care needs. Are the residents clean, neatly groomed, and tastefully attired?

Observe medication administration. Is this done by a licensed nurse? Are medications and residents checked to make sure that

Making the Decision | 29

the residents get the correct medicine and dosages? Does the nurse take time to make sure the residents have their questions regarding the medication answered and that they receive the help they need to take them?

When you notice that the nursing staff is responding quickly, appropriately, carefully, and compassionately, you have an indication that the facility is carrying out the medical component.

Are the television sets in good repair? Are there VCRs, record players, tape decks, and other entertainment equipment? Is there a schedule of activities posted for everyone to see? Do you notice residents engaged in group and solitary activities? Are rooms available for the residents' use for lounging, watching TV, visiting, or engaging in group recreation? Are there appropriate seasonal decorations throughout the facility? If all this is in place, you realize that the facility is meeting the recreational part of their many-pronged program.

Do you see many residents up and out of their rooms? Are those who do not walk, sitting up? Is there a room where residents are obviously working with professionals on improving their strength, flexibility, ambulation, and self-help skills? Do you note that residents are encouraged to do all that they can do for themselves even though it might be easier to do it for them? Are rehabilitation assistants helping residents in their own rooms engage in range of motion exercises? You will probably not see the speech therapist in action as that therapy is performed behind closed doors so as not to embarrass or distract the residents. Do look at the rehabilitation portion of the program.

Does the dining room look good to you? Is it clean and comfortable? Are residents seated in chairs rather than rolled up to the tables in wheelchairs? Some residents will want to stay in their wheelchairs but many feel better when transferred to a regular dining room chair. It makes the meal more of an event and the residents more sociable. Is the menu posted and alternative food selections listed? Everybody cannot like or eat everything, and a chance to choose is appreciated. Does the food look and smell like something you would like to eat? If you perceive all the above to be true, the restaurant piece is in place.

The social worker may be the first person you meet when you visit the nursing home. Does he or she look like someone you can talk to? Is he or she able to explain processes and procedures in an understandable way? As he or she walks through the hallways, do the residents seem to know him or her and seem happy to see him or her? Is the social worker's office designed for your comfort? Is it appointed in a way that makes you feel they want you to be in a place that shows that the facility values its residents and their families? Are you given the opportunity to talk in private? Do you get the idea that any question you ask will be answered graciously and candidly? If you answer yes, you are saying that the nursing home is providing mental health and emotional support services.

One part may be more important to you and your relative, depending on the relative's needs. If there is sickness the medical aspects are more dominant in your mind. If there are emotional problems you are more concerned regarding the social service department. Perhaps rehabilitation is your goal. If the relative is healthy and alert your focus may be on recreational opportunities. Your priorities may change as the resident's needs change. All are important. Find the nursing home able to meet needs as the needs change.

Feel

Every place has an ambience. Some places make you feel excited, others, soothed. Sometimes you dislike a place for no apparent reason. There seems to be something in the environment that creates a negative emotion. Other times and other locations may elicit a positive reaction. If your feeling about the nursing home is either negative or positive look for the evidence that created the feeling.

Unfortunately, a negative impact is not uncommon when visiting a nursing home. The many disoriented, handicapped residents are a distressing sight. Many facilities have taken steps to negate this blow by providing beautiful offices, entry ways, and reception areas with soothing and coordinated colors, elegant but serviceable furniture and fabrics, and richly appointed common rooms. This does help. Being in lovely surroundings enhances the residents' good feelings about themselves. It is nice to be in a place that is admired by all.

Older nursing homes that have been established for a long time may not have the floor space to provide the decorative cushion for the visitor prior to their coming in contact with the residents. The visitor may instead be greeted by the occupants as soon as they enter the door.

If you feel good about the decor and sad about the residents, try to separate the feelings and focus on the appearance of the residents instead of the appearance of the residence.

Many residents out of their rooms and interacting in a noisy, friendly way may seem overwhelming, and prompting an initial feeling of chaos. Try to look closer. This generally is a sign that the facility staff is amicable and stimulating and the residents are a major part of day-to-day activities.

Nursing homes with a quiet, room-bound populace may give you a feeling of serenity when instead it has a sterile and stifling atmosphere.

Feelings about the physical environment and the residents are important. So are your feelings about the staff. If you feel they are happy to be with you, your relative will get the same feeling. You do want people pleasers in positions that require resident contact. The medical records clerk may be a grouch, and that's all right. You want to see pleasantness in the nursing assistants, the activities coordinator, the social worker, and all those people who will be working with your relative. At the same time that you are feeling relieved and lighter-hearted, you also should get an impression about the competence of the staff. Do you feel they know what they are doing? Do they act as if they like and know their jobs?

Facts

Charges

The room and board fee for nursing home care is high. When initially presented it generally brings a gasp. To put it in perspective, it does not cost as much as a room in a good hotel and it is less expensive than around-the-clock nursing care in the home. It does include all meals and snacks, the attentions of all the skilled staff, personal care, counseling, individual and group activities, housekeeping, medical monitoring, and routine restorative approaches. Extra charges are levied for medication, doctor visits, personal laundry, special diets such as liquid nutrition, hair salon costs, medical transportation, and physical, speech, and occupational therapy. Find out exactly what is included in the basic rate and what the additional costs will be. This should be spelled out very specifically in the admissions contract.

Although costs may vary from home to home, select the place you and your relative like rather than the one with the lowest rate. Not that money is not a consideration. It obviously is, but no elderly nursing home residents will go without the needed care even if they have no funds. This is because of the Medicaid program. This is a question to concern you at the time of exploration. Even though your relative may be able to pay for the care initially, funds quickly dissipate unless the resident has a high monthly income that covers the cost. All nursing homes that are authorized to receive Medicaid are not allowed, by law, to evict a resident when they can no longer pay from their private funds and must apply to the state for Medicaid coverage. The nursing home staff will help with the application by directing you and your relative in the proper procedure. Question them as to their policy of notification and assistance. Discuss finances frankly. They cannot give you the information you need if they do not know that you need it.

Briefly, Medicaid is a tax-supported program administered by the state. It differs somewhat from state to state. Medicaid assistance can begin the first day of nursing home care or after the residents' own funds are depleted. Application for coverage is made through the State Health and Welfare Department in the county where the resident resides. It is based on need. The resident's income, assets, expenses, and medical condition are the basis for determining eligibility. Relatives, including children, siblings, and spouses, are not legally responsible for payment for the resident's care nor is their financial status considered in the determination of the resident's resources. However, funds and assets jointly owned by the resident and anyone else are considered available to the resident and listed in the credit column. Because of this, assets should be separated as people grow older and the possibility of the nursing home looms. Check for further details with your local State Health and Welfare Department.

Residents covered by Medicaid are not charged extra for any of their medical care and will receive a small monthly allowance to use to pay for other charges and for their personal use.

There are other sources for nursing home payment. Insurance companies sell long-term-care insurance. It is crucial to determine if they pay for unskilled or custodial care because this is the type of care that goes on the longest and is not covered by Medicare. Many companies will not sell long-term-care insurance to people over eighty or to those with serious health problems. Since this is the case, it is wise to look into coverage before it is needed. So far, nursing homes have been leery about a resident's having this coverage because the policies seem to be restrictive. Because of this, do not rely solely on the salesperson's interpretation of coverage. Double-check with the company, with other insurance experts, and with an accountant who understands insurance policies.

Medicare pays for nursing home care, but not as much as people expect or hope. It is quite restricted, covering only certain medical conditions and for a limited period of time. It is not something residents can rely on for as long as they need nursing home care. Another concern with Medicare coverage is that nursing homes are required to designate Medicare beds in the facility. Consequently, when a resident is no longer receiving Medicare coverage he or she must be moved to a non-Medicare bed, which can be any other location in the facility. The beds and the rooms may be identical, but the move may be unwanted by the resident.

The Veterans Administration pays for needed nursing home care for veterans receiving disability. At this writing they will pay any nursing home the veteran selects if the nursing home has an agreement with the Veterans Administration. Not all nursing homes have signed or will sign this agreement. If the prospective resident is a disabled veteran, appraise the latest policies and procedures with the local Veterans Administration officer and determine which nursing homes work with them.

If nursing homes in your area are crowded and have resorted to waiting lists you should know that waiting lists do not mean that the applicant will be admitted when the name comes to the top of the list. The first taken are those who can pay the full fee and those with medical conditions that do not require time-consuming and difficult procedures. They will take residents from hospitals before they take them from home. This means that if you are thinking of nursing home placement think of placing directly from the hospital. And, since Medicaid does not pay the full nursing home fee, plan to pay privately when the resident first enters the nursing home if you want a speedier admission. If the residents have physical problems that require skilled nursing and qualify for Medicare payment in the nursing home, plan nursing home care before this benefit is terminated. Medicare is considered as good as private payments, known in the industry as "private pay." By the same token, if you and your relative don't like the nursing home, transfer to another while the resident is covered by Medicare or is paying privately.

To summarize, the residents easiest to place in a nursing home are those who

1. Pay privately / Medicare.
2. Are in the hospital.
3. Need uncomplicated nursing care.

In the nursing home there are three levels of care. They are:
SKILLED: Medicare coverage is for skilled care only. This is for people who need twenty-four-hour medical supervision and special treatment by a registered nurse for a physical problem.

INTERMEDIATE: No special medical procedure is required, but the residents need medical attention. They are unable to live alone.

CUSTODIAL: No special medical attention is required, but supervision and assistance with the tasks of daily living are needed.

Medical Care

In spite of all its roles, a nursing home is a medical facility. All residents are expected, at one time or another, to need medical care. The majority of the staff are medically oriented. Those that are not are called ancillary staff. Policies and procedures, rules and regulations, are geared to the medical. The director of nursing has a power position in the facility. Residents are known as patients because of the medical orientation. In fact, many of the people living in nursing homes are patients and need constant medical supervision. Care follows the medical model. Nothing can be done, including activities, without an order from the physician. Patient is probably the correct label for those who live in nursing homes. They are referred to as residents by the author because the name resident has a more positive connotation. Patient implies sickness and being cared for. Others are responsible for a patient. Good patients do as those in medical authority say they should do. Residents, in contrast, signify people who are living in a place, have a free will, and can think and plan for themselves. Residents can have physical problems. That does not mean that they have lost their personal identity and are nothing more than a health concern. The average length of stay in a nursing home is three years. That is a long time to give over your life to medical care. It is better to see people who live in nursing homes as residents who live there because the facility offers what they need at that time in their lives.

STAFFING Registered or licensed practical nurses must be assigned to each duty station around the clock. Nursing homes are required to have a certain number of nurses and assistants on duty for a given number of residents. Consequently, nursing home staffing either meets or exceeds staffing requirements. The more staff available to assist the residents, the more likely it will be that the resident receives attention promptly. Nursing homes have to meet minimum staffing standards to be licensed. If they exceed these standards they will be glad you asked about staffing patterns and proud to give you this information. *This is one of your more important questions.* Everybody in the facility may want to do a good job, but if there are not enough people (understaffed) to do it, the intentions will not show up in the results.

You will want to know that there are adequate ancillary staff as well. Nursing staff needs to be free to attend to their nursing duties. This occurs only if the Activity, Social Service, Maintenance, Housekeeping, Restorative, Administrative, and Dietary departments have a full complement of people. The nursing home staff will be pleased to let you know of their varied services and staff available to assist you and the resident.

You might inquire as to how the nursing staff is assigned to the residents. Some long-term-care facilities are doing primary nursing. This means that a team of nursing staff is assigned a certain number of designated residents. This team cares for those residents for a period of one to eight months before shifting to be primarily responsible for a different group of residents for a set period of time. It is difficult to schedule staff for these kinds of assignments as the around-the-clock staff have to have times that mesh so that the caregivers can remain the same for the residents.

Primary nursing has been good for both residents and staff. Each identify with the other. A mutual closeness develops. They learn each other's ways. There is less anxiety and agitation and more trust. This means there are fewer physical and chemical restraints. Disoriented residents feel more secure and less threatened when they see the same people day after day. Better resident grooming is noted as the assigned nursing staff is more familiar with the residents' wardrobes and take pride in "their" residents looking their best. Families become more equal and contributing members of the team as they work more closely with their relatives' caregivers. Staff can be assigned to residents based on personality and ability.

There are negatives as difficult residents can contribute to staff burnout. There tend to be more mutual attachments. Change of staff or death of a resident can cause a state of grief because of the closeness that occurred over the time they worked together.

PHYSICIAN VISITS Physicians are mandated to examine each nursing home resident they follow, record their findings, and sign their orders every thirty to forty-five days. There are doctors who are willing to visit the facility to carry out this procedure. Since there are few physicians who go to nursing homes on a regular basis, one or two physicians who do go there see many, if not most, of the residents who live there. This does not mean that your relative has to use the available nursing home doctor. This means that there is a doctor who will probably accept your relative as a patient since he or she goes to the facility anyway. The residents may elect to go to the offices of the doctor of their choice. If transportation can be arranged and they are physically able to manage the trip, the residents frequently prefer this as they feel the care is more personalized, more private, they can continue with a doctor they've known for some time (and who knows them), and it gives them an opportunity for an outing.

If you and your relative decide to hire the facility physician you will want to make sure he or she understands all your medical concerns and will abide by your and your relative's wishes.

Medical specialists are also necessary. Although you can not expect that every specialist will make regular visits to the nursing home, you will want to ask which specialties are represented. If your relatives find it difficult to get around, going to the offices of several physicians is more than they may be able or willing to do. If the doctors do not go to the home, aspects of resident health may be neglected. So ask. Which doctors regularly come to the facility? Some that are important are the podiatrist, the dentist, the ophthamologist, or the optometrist. Feet, teeth, and eye care on a regular basis prevents many problems. It is part of the restorative approach as it helps maintain the residents' well-being and their ability to get around, chew, and see.

A LIVING WILL If the prospective nursing home residents have living wills and have a written document that states their wishes about life-prolonging medical procedures when their medical condition is hopeless, you will want to make sure that the doctor and the nursing home will honor this statement. Some states have passed proxy laws that enable residents to designate a friend or family member to make health-care decisions for them if they are unable to do so. Preplanning with relatives before this becomes a necessity will enable you to follow their wishes when they can no longer make them known. Make a copy of the living will and/or the proxy available to the doctor and the nursing home. Make sure it is on the resident's chart. If the living will is a meaningful directive, query the nursing home policy in this regard. Be sure they do not have policies that keep them from following living will instructions.

FINAL ARRANGEMENTS Many people avoid nursing homes because they see them as a place people go to die, and can cite numerous examples of that happening. Consequently, the inevitable question by the nursing home admissions coordinator requesting the preferred funeral home is a real downer. The fact is that this is a practical question that gives the facility the information they need in order to carry out your wishes and plans. It is also a time for you to help your relative make a decision that may earlier have been avoided.

TECHNOLOGY As people live longer, more people grow old enough to suffer from Alzheimer's disease. With each decade of age there is more of a possibility of the incidence of the disease. Thus, nursing home staff find it increasingly necessary to cater to the particular problems of the Alzheimer's resident. These problems include agitation, disorientation, and wandering away. In other words, the resident with Alzheimer's may unwittingly get into dangerous situations because of misinterpreting social cues, feeling threatened when no threat is there, going unbidden into other residents' rooms, and walking off from the facility. Restrictions have been placed on the use of physical restraints that prevent the disruptive and unsafe behavior in which the Alzheimer's resident can engage. Staff members have had to use other methods to curb the unwanted behavior. Medication can help but is also closely monitored. Chemical restraints in the form of drugs are not approved. Staff members' vigilance is important, as are locked and alarmed doors. Additionally, facilities are turning to the use of electronics to signal when a person is in the wrong area. These electronics can be in the form of a wrist or ankle bracelet, are nonintrusive, and are conducive to the residents' security. Do ask what safeguards the facility uses to prevent perilous circumstances.

FAMILY NOTIFICATION Question the staff of the nursing home regarding their policy and procedure for family notification. Give them names, addresses, and telephone numbers. Keep this information up-to-date, and make sure it is posted where the night shift nurse will look when an emergency arises. Usually the front of the resident's medical chart is the best place, but the social worker and the bookkeeper should also be kept current.

It is not reasonable to expect that staff will call several family members, or that they will continually convey minutiae. It is totally reasonable to expect to be notified about health problems and room changes. If you have an interest in being specifically told of other occurrences, write out what you want to know, determine who is to notify you, and make sure your request is posted where all staff will see it. Make social services as well as nursing aware of your wishes.

Let the staff know who is the designated person to be notified, when that person is available, and whom to call if that person cannot be reached.

RESTORATION A long-term-care facility provides nursing care. It should also provide rehabilitation. You may question this statement, knowing that your relatives are physically unable to return to their former full capabilities and may be terminal. This does not mean that they cannot do certain things for themselves. The rehabilitative or restorative approach in a nursing home emphasizes that all get the opportunity to be all that they can be in every area of living—physical, emotional, and social. The restorative approach means that residents feel like residents, not patients. They are encouraged to exert their free wills, state preferences, make choices, and have their wishes respected and acted on. This restorative philosophy is one that treats the residents as the adults they are, and as people who have control over their own lives. They are given opportunities to belong, to engage in self-governing activities, to feel equal to the caregiving staff, to learn adaptive techniques for managing activities of daily living, and to feel good about themselves.

Nursing homes have a restorative nurse on their staff who sets up a program that assists with the above as well as teaches self-help skills and works at maintaining physical abilities. Restorative approaches are included in team-care plans for all residents. You will want to be part of the restorative approach. You will want to ask if every department is dedicated to the restorative practice.

Room Change Policies

Residents rent space in a nursing home. They do not rent a certain bed in a certain room. Because the nursing home population is constantly changing there is also a constant rearranging of where the residents live. They come and go. Their physical and mental conditions change. They have disagreements and fallings out with roommates. It is a rare thing for one resident to keep one bed in one place over a long period of time. This is not a good situation for many residents. The disoriented become more so if they have to try to learn a new location again and again. Many residents simply find a move disturbing.

Residents go home, go to hospitals, and die. This leaves empty beds to rent to incoming residents. If a prospective resident is male and the empty bed is in a room with a female, changes will have to be made. If roommates do not get along and request a move, their wishes must be accommodated. If one person moves, another must, too. Residents who get sick and need skilled nursing may have to be moved to a different section of the facility. It seems as though none of this can be avoided.

Nevertheless, you will want to be notified in ample time of any proposed room change so you and your relative can adjust to the eventuality or state your case if you are adamantly opposed. If your relative is disoriented, you will want to make every effort to prevent a move.

Nursing home staff members do endeavor to avoid disrupting the residents. At the same time, they have to make changes to honor requests, for residents' safety, for health reasons, and to make room for new residents. Help them see why they should not cause distress to your relative. And do find out about the facility's philosophy regarding room changes.

MISCELLANEOUS

Concerns

You and your loved one who may one day face nursing home placement should discuss what you know and have heard about nursing homes in the area you want to consider. Talk to people who have had experience. Get as many impressions as you can. People are only too happy to provide comments and opinions. After you gather all the information, sort through it to see if there is a pattern. Find out if the complaint is current. There will always be some isolated complaints that are not necessarily significant. Some horror stories are carried forward from years ago when there were different staff members and more lenient regulatory bodies. Much of what you hear you will want to ignore. A nursing home is, after all, not like home or like a hospital. It is a nursing home. Care is delivered on schedule. As much as staff may try to accommodate an individual's wishes, they are generally unable to deviate too much from what has to be accomplished by a certain time. Unless you hear stories of neglect and abuse and a pattern emerges, you may want to discount much of what comes your way.

Listen most carefully to complaints of recent problems such as

1. Discourteous, uncaring staff members
2. Abuse
3. Neglect
4. Poor maintenance
5. Uncleanliness

Any of these concerns may make you decide to cross that facility off your list. If you like the nursing home, but you've heard a complaint, you should discuss it with the admissions coordinator, social worker, or administrator. It may be the first time they know of the problem, or the problem may be based on a misunderstanding. What you want to know is whether they address the problem, deny it, or dismiss it as unimportant. Nursing home staff members that share your concern and want to hear about and correct what is wrong are the ones you can work with. You know they will respond and try to make improvements as they are needed. If you get a positive reaction to your complaint you will want to consider the facility as a good possibility for placement.

Do not be surprised if the facility staff state that they cannot discuss a specific complaint with you, but give general information instead. This is because nursing home residents are guaranteed confidentiality. Staff members are bound by law not to disclose private and personal information about any nursing home resident. Do not consider them evasive, but realize they are upholding the residents' rights to confidentiality.

Preferences

If your relative has preferences (and who doesn't?), make them clear to nursing home staff at the time of admission. Make note of whether or not the staff members want to hear what the resident wants and how far they are able or willing to go to accommodate individual differences. The residents should be encouraged to express their wishes and have their desires respected in the following areas:

- Preferred form of address
- Use of personal items in decorating and furnishing the room
- Supervision of room cleaning
- Responsibility for dresser drawers and closet cleaning
- Bathroom lights left on or off
- Time of arising and retiring
- Nap times
- Snack times and preferred snacks
- Visitor schedules
- Bath times
- Tub or shower bath
- Frequency of hair-care appointments
- Meals in the dining room or in the resident's room
- Events to celebrate
- In room or group activities
- Outdoor excursions
- Newspaper delivery
- Community activities
- In room telephone
- Any other thing you or your relative think is important

In summary:

1. Check to see if the nursing home and the administrator are licensed.

2. Ask about the cost. What does the rate include? What are usual additional expenses? How much is covered by Medicare, Medicaid, Veterans Administration funds, or private insurance? When do charges start and stop? Will there be a refund if the resident does not stay for an entire month? How will the resident's Medicaid allowance for personal needs be handled?

3. Does the nursing home reserve the resident's bed for him or her when he or she leaves for a mandatory hospital stay or a visit with relatives? Is the resident charged for time away from the home?

4. Do residents have a voice on who their roommate will be? Are residents able to stay in the same room for an indefinite

period of time, or are they moved for administrative convenience?

5. Is the facility near family, friends, doctor, and the hospital? What are the visiting hours?

6. Visit the home. How does it smell? Is it clean? Is it cheerfully furnished? Are there handrails along the hallway? How is the temperature? Look into the nonpublic areas; does the kitchen look as if it is sanitary? Are there safety features?

7. Talk to the nursing home residents. Are they cheerful? Do they like the staff? Are they pleased with their care? Sample the food.

8. Ask if any special services are provided, such as a barber or a hairdresser. Do the residents ever leave the home for outings?

9. What kind of activities are planned on a regular basis? Ask for a copy of the activity calendar. What is done to encourage the new resident to participate?

10. Does the nursing home have a volunteer program? Many volunteers are a sign of healthy community involvement and a busy program of recreation and entertainment.

11. Ask about the staff. How many nurses are usually on duty? What are their training and experience? What other staff are employed to care for the resident? Talk to some of the staff. Are they open, friendly, concerned?

12. What pharmacy do they use? How are medications packaged? Is it a problem if you want to have prescriptions filled by a different pharmacy?

13. Is the contract clear to you? If not, have a staff member explain it to you or take it to an attorney.

MAKING THE ADJUSTMENT

Adapting to change is always difficult. With every decision something is gained, something is lost. When the nursing home placement decision is made, security and safety are gained, privacy and independence are lost. As much as nursing home staff struggle to help residents be as independent as they can be and honor their privacy, group living is dramatically different from living alone or with family. Adjustment does not come easily for the residents or the residents' families.

When the residents are dealt with forthrightly and included in the decision process as much as possible steps have been taken that aid in a positive adjustment. The more involved the residents can be in making the choice the more satisfied they will be with the result. If it is done to them they feel powerless. If it is done with them they have a sense of control. Feeling some control makes an overwhelming situation less so. Moving into a foreign setting when coping skills are weakened by physical and mental impairments complicates a difficult experience. If they feel no part of the decision they reject it. They fight against it. Adjustment is impossible. If they make the decision with the help of others they assist in making it work. Adjustment is possible.

This does not mean that adjustment is painless. That cannot be. It is not easy. It is not without problems. Adjustment may not be rapid or move in a straight line from distress to complete acceptance. It is not all bad until it is suddenly good. Adjustment is a process. The pain is experienced. There are setbacks, disappointments, and many things to dislike. It is gradual. It is something that can be accomplished.

Coping with Stress

If mom, dad, husband, or wife has always had difficulty adjusting to change and traumatic events you can be sure they will fall back on their old patterns of behavior. Those that exhibited flexibility, adaptive skills, and good coping ability will use these strengths again.

If your relative always blamed others for problems, you will be blamed when the relative moves into a nursing home. This time, do not take the blame. Instead, realize that no blame is warranted. What was done was simply what had to be done.

If your relative manipulated others to take responsibility and make decisions for him or her, this pattern will again emerge. Since you have probably been part of this performance in the past, you can easily fall prey to old habits. Change your ways. Confront your relative with the choices. If you must make the decisions, explain what they are and why they are being made. Give opportunity for disagreements or other suggestions. Make sure that the relative realizes that since you are making the decision at his or her request you expect him or her to be satisfied with what you decide.

If your relative became depressed when losses occurred, your relative will again exhibit these symptoms. They may include changes in eating and sleeping habits, complaints of physical problems, crying, irritability, negativity, hopelessness, helplessness, withdrawal, slowness in thought, and complaints of poor memory.

Depression related to change is not unusual. It ameliorates as the adjustment is made. You can be helpful by being supportive, encouraging, and available. Try to get your relative involved in the nursing home routine. Ask the activity coordinator to invite your relative to recreational events; ask the social worker to explore concerns. You may want an evaluation for antidepressant medication from a physician and counseling to help your relative overcome the depression.

If your relative was critical and complaining don't expect a change when nursing home placement occurs. You can plan on hearing continuous complaints about the routine, the staff, the organization, and the amenities of the facility. If you have always listened and tried to fix whatever your relative saw was wrong you will be relied upon to do so again.

Since you know your relative's penchant for being critical, accept all reports, but do not take them as something that has to be acted on. Hear the complaints. Get as much information as you can. You may want to discuss some of the concerns with appropriate staff, but do so in a fact-finding, not accusatory, way. Don't let your relative play on your guilt. Guilt will cause you to overreact and try to take care of a problem that may not actually be one. When possible, slip in good words about the staff and the services and in a small, inconspicuous way help your relative develop a more positive attitude. In the meantime, seeing the good parts of what is happening will help you too. If you focus solely on your relative's complaints, your visit and your outlook will be negative. This is not good for you or the resident.

If your relative has handled stress by becoming physically ill, be wary of this reaction again. If you always gave extra attention and sympathy at those times be prepared to do so again. However, let the nursing home staff know of this pattern. You can help by giving less attention to the physical symptoms and more attention to the emotional impact of the nursing home adjustment. Get your relative to externalize the fears and anxieties by talking about them instead of expressing them in physical laments. You can do this by commenting on what is happening, asking questions about feelings, and talking about nursing home events and routines. Of course, you will not minimize the physical distress. You will simply reflect on the emotional impact of change.

The adjustment to a new and strange living condition takes time. It takes time for you as well as for your relative. Do not expect your relative to assist you in your adjustment to this dramatic and emotion-producing change. Take care of yourself. When you can deal with your emotions you can manage your relative's emotions constructively and without debilitating guilt. If you cannot do this alone, accept that fact and get help. Talk with the nursing home social worker or make an appointment for counseling.

Medical Attention

Pain and suffering take precedence over everything. People cannot think good thoughts, welcome new experiences, or develop positive outlooks when energy and attention are drained by physical agony. Do not naively encourage them to ignore their symptoms or to make the best of it. Instead, focus your energy and attention on physical relief. Make sure your relative's physician knows of the health problems and treats them aggressively, issuing orders for pain medication and rehabilitation therapies as needed. If the resident feels that effective medical care is available the anxiety will lessen, hope will rise, and the adjustment will proceed. If pain and suffering cannot be alleviated, the resident can handle it better if he or she knows what is going on and is assured that everything that can be done is being done.

The medical staff of the nursing home cannot stop the aging process, cure incurable diseases, or provide relief from all physical discomfort. You and your relative have to accept this. When the resident has been provided with all the help there is you will be of more assistance if you can let go and deal with reality. But if you continue to question and seek different answers you put pressure on your relative to somehow be better than is possible, to be stronger, to get healthier. You delay adjustment for yourself and the resident.

Social Supports

People can be lonely in a crowd. Nursing home residents are surrounded by others. This does not assuage loneliness for a new resident. The ones they are lonely for are those who gave life meaning before this unnerving move to a nursing home. You can help in the adjustment by continuing to give attention and time. You demonstrate by calls and visits that the resident is not abandoned, you have not lost interest, and your contacts will remain at a workable level. This does not mean that you will spend every waking moment at the facility. That does not aid adjustment as it prevents the residents from acclimating to new surroundings and routines. Although you may spend more time with your relative during the adjustment phase, make it clear that you will be planning regular visits, less frequently, in the future.

At the same time that you are giving time and attention to aid the resident in transition, encourage other relatives and friends to make contact. You may have to sell them on the idea that they can make a difference, that the resident needs and appreciates them, and that the resident is still a part of their lives. Too many people see those in nursing homes as dropouts from society and do not continue their support. The residents have not died. They have changed where they live. They still need love and belonging.

While you continue to keep your relative interested in life

outside the facility, do not monopolize the time and attention to such an extent that he or she does not develop an interest in what goes on in the nursing home. You want to be part of your relative's life, not your relative's whole life.

Play a Part in Planning

If there is no choice regarding nursing home placement do not pretend that there is. Explain what is happening and why. Give choices only when you can. Do you want nursing home A or B? Do you want a bed by the door or the window? Do you want to go by car or by ambulance? Do you want to take your television set? Get participation. Whenever your relative can give needed information to the nursing home staff have her or him, and not you, do it. The more she or he is involved and the more decisions she or he makes in regard to the placement, the more the mind-set moves toward placement instead of against placement. You are not helping your relative by protecting him or her. People can handle situations if they know what the situation is. They cannot cope when they do not have the necessary information. As painful as it may be, include your relative in the entire process, stepping in to take care of only what she or he cannot manage. People want to know all about that which affects them personally.

You may decide that the thought of nursing home placement is too upsetting for your relative to handle. Your fears may be confirmed when she or he is, indeed, supremely distressed when placement is proposed to her or him. This distraught state is nothing compared to what will happen to you and the relative if placement is thrust upon him or her. Adjustment will be delayed, if not completely thwarted. It is better if you allow the prospective resident to air the misery as it happens than to compound it and have it as a reaction to what has happened. Everyone has a right to know what is going on that concerns them and to have feelings about it. Allow the feelings and help the prospective resident express and handle the feelings.

Honesty

There may be a tactful way to explain the inevitability of nursing home placement to a relative. It is fine to use tact, to be diplomatic, to be considerate. But nothing takes the place of the truth. No matter how sick, disoriented, or uncooperative people are, they still need to be told the truth. Some of the saddest circumstances are those of residents who cannot adjust to nursing home living—they are always planning and waiting to go home. If residents are led to believe that they are continuing in a medical setting and will go home after a short stay they rightfully expect that to happen. They do not get involved in nursing home life, develop relationships, take an interest in activities, or occupy themselves in anything that interferes with their intended leaving after a short stay. Disoriented residents who cannot remember anything that happened yesterday will remember that they are to go home. They will spend hours waiting at the door for the event to take place. A simple lie used to prevent pain contributes to an ongoing maladjustment that is impossible to remedy unless the truth is finally told. The pain has to be experienced then, and the adjustment finally begun.

Just remember that it is easier to be truthful all along than to live a lie. The lie prevents your relative from living as well as he or she can and compromises your relationship, which is then built on a lie. The relative will constantly badger you to take him or her home. You will have to keep lying. Misery compounds. Be honest. Be free.

Timely and Usable Information

You can assist your relative by giving information as you know it in a way that makes sense. Your relative will not realize that he or she has to make a nursing home selection if he or she cannot understand why. A person does not know how to select one facility over another unless he or she knows what to look for. No one will be able to adjust to a new physician unless he or she learns why it is not possible to continue with the family's tried and true medical doctor. Give your relative the needed information prior to the deadline so he or she can get used to the idea and adjust to the necessity of a decision. Give enough data that a decision can be made. Answer questions, discuss alternatives, and provide facts. As you do this you are reinforcing strengths and assisting the adjustment.

Assistance

Anybody who has ever tried to follow written instructions to program a VCR, sew a shirt, or assemble a bicycle knows the feeling of hopelessness when it cannot be made to go the way the diagram shows it should go. Assistance that is provided at the right time, and that leads to success, enhances self-esteem, reinstills hope, and ensures a feeling of competence.

You can help your relative by giving assistance at the right time so it will lead to success. When he or she feels the weakest and most vulnerable you can be there to help. This means that you can teach her or him the nursing home schedule, learn who does what, where your relative is allowed to smoke, if he or she can have cereal for breakfast, and how to manage the situation with a difficult resident or staff member. You cannot change the particulars. You can guide. You can step in to assist in a tough spot. Your relative can be more effective if you empower her or him with your support, strength, and help. You do not do it for her or him. You help him or her be more effective by stepping in at the right time. For example:

Mrs. M did not know what to do. She enjoyed getting out of her room to eat in the dining room, but could not cope with one of her table companions who took food off Mrs. M's plate. The other resident did not stop when she was chastised. Staff members did not notice it. Mrs. M did not want to make trouble. She decided she would eat in her room. When her daughter discovered her mother with a lunch tray she learned what had happened. Mrs. M was feeling angry, impotent, and hurt. The daughter asked the social worker to come in to talk with them. With the daughter's support, Mrs. M explained her problem. The food snatcher was seated elsewhere, where there was more supervision. Mrs. M returned to the dining room with a feeling of success. It gave her more confidence to deal with future reversals.

Adjustment Reactions

Stress happens. Change, loss, hassles, both large and small, traumatic and unpredictable events, all occur. Moving to a nursing home encompasses all that. A stress reaction is normal and expected. You will note in your relative the symptoms of stress. Some of them are regression, denial, hostility, immobility, anxiety, and physical symptoms.

Regression

When under stress regression as a reaction is a common phenomenon. It often occurs automatically when confronted with stern authority, when adjusting to new situations, in medical facilities, and in the classroom environment. Nursing home residents have more than one reason to regress. They are in medical surroundings, physicians and nurses are seen as authority figures, and the circumstances are new and ruffling.

Regression is not an altogether bad response. If used only for acclimatization it is useful. It allows residents time to gather strength while they survey their surroundings, determine where they fit in, and figure out how to deal with what they see.

Regression is detrimental if it becomes a way of life. Unfortunately, the stage is set for this to happen. Nursing home staff are caring and are caregivers. Many see their value in what they can do for people. A nursing home is a medical facility and the word nursing implies constant attention. Those admitted are labeled patients. Patients need care, are supposed to do as they are told, not question their caregivers, and comply with a medical regimen. You and the staff can help your relative by guarding against this medical mentality.

If your relative wheeled his or her own wheelchair before placement, encourage her or him to continue. If he or she bathed without help, attended to his or her own grooming, or made her or his own choice of attire, insist that that continue. He or she may need help. The help should be to assist the resident to do all he or she can do and be all that he or she can be.

Regression can result in more dependency. The nursing home staff's job is to inspire residents to more independence. You can promote this by asking your relative to continue in activities and projects he or she pursued prior to placement and to function as independently as possible. Ask her or him to crochet a doily, assemble a birdhouse, write letters, make telephone calls, or be part of the facility's volunteer program.

Do not misinterpret the staff's urging the residents to self-help as unwillingness to do their job. See this as an important part of their job.

Denial

When stress is overwhelming, a not unusual defense is to deny what is happening. Cancer patients can pretend they have the flu or nursing home residents can deny they are there permanently or even deny they are in a nursing home. An unpleasant confrontation is not necessary, but it is not helpful to go along with the residents' denial. Staff members will not be unkind, but they will remind the residents where they are and explain that the facility is their home. You can follow suit. When the residents become more comfortable in their surroundings they are more able to face the truth.

Hostility

In spite of careful planning in which the residents' choices and wishes are adhered to, anger at the results may still occur. Your relative may be angry that he or she is in a nursing home and make you the brunt of the hostile behavior. If you are greeted by a wrathful relative at every contact, visits are unpleasant. You may be made to feel guilty, or you may feel angry in return. You may want to avoid seeing your relative. It is easier on you if the staff members endure the ire as they are more likely to be dispassionate and not take the disagreeable behavior personally. Neither outlet for the resident's anger is constructive, nor should they take it out on themselves.

The best help you can give is to let your relative talk about the anger, listen, and accept. Do not get defensive. Do not try to justify. Let him or her get it out. On the other hand, if you point out how he or she is wrong, he or she will have to think of more reasons for his or her opinion and intensify his or her position. Instead, simply acknowledge that most people would be upset at having to leave their own homes. You are on your relative's side.

You understand. Do not argue back. Keep telling yourself that you aided your relative in doing what had to be done. You do not have to feel guilty.

If the anger is justifiable, say so. If there is anything that can be done about the situation that is making the resident angry, see that it is done. For example, Mr. N was furious that the nursing assistant wanted him to eat breakfast. Mr. N had never eaten breakfast, but liked a midmorning snack. His relative could help him negotiate that with the nursing home staff so he did not have to concentrate on that aggravation.

Pick up on positives. Whenever the relative notes something he or she likes, a person he or she enjoyed, an experience, or anything affirmative, reward him or her with attention, approval, and pleasure. The good feelings that result from your generous demeanor reinforce a more favorable outlook.

If anger continues, you may want to make arrangements for your relative to talk with a counselor so he or she may work through the feelings and get on with life.

If all else fails and your relative seems stuck in anger, you may have to go over the reasons for nursing home placement, the fact that there are no alternative plans, and point out that you do not want to hear about it anymore as there is nothing you can do to change the situation. Explain that you are also distressed, want him or her to be happy, and you want to enjoy his or her company. Suggest subjects you would like to talk about. Distract him or her with topics in which he or she is interested. Involve her or him in activities that do not leave time for animosity.

Immobility

Change may be so stressful that the new resident may be immobilized. Any who have experienced a traumatic change or loss may be unable to proceed until they adjust. The adjustment involves learning a new lifestyle. When surroundings and schedules are all changed, sensibilities suffer. The normal thinking, acting, and feeling processes need realignment. For a time it may be that the residents cannot concentrate, decide, or remember. They may be unable to proceed with putting their belongings away, arranging them to their needs, and locating them when they want them. Who does what? When are they supposed to be where? They may not be able to remember their roommate's name. They may refuse to leave their room. They may not want to get dressed. It is a good time for you to provide a stable and steadying influence. Some nursing home staff will recommend that family not visit until the residents are settled into the new routine. Do not take their advice. Be with your relative frequently over the first week. He or she needs to know that everything has not changed. You will be an anchor for her or him. Give an assist in stowing the belongings. Give him or her opportunities to make small decisions on where he or she wants certain possessions. Accompany your relative to a couple of nursing home events. Take him or her on an orientation tour of the facility. Engage staff members in conversation in your relative's presence. Get to know your relative's roommate. Take your relative out for lunch, a ride, a visit if he or she can go, and then back to the new home. This makes the facility feel more like a place to live rather than a place of confinement.

Anxiety

Tension is normal in a new situation. Everyone experiences a surge to the system when feeling nervous in an unfamiliar setting. This will occur with recent admissions to a nursing home. Normal amounts of anxiety are to be expected. The problem exists when the anxiety becomes disabling. The anxiety attacks that are frightening and debilitating result in physical symptoms which may include rapid and/or missed heartbeats and/or a heavy feeling in the chest, pain, tremors, tightness in the throat, dizziness, stomach upset, headache, and vision problems. New residents who have had such episodes in the past will have a recurrence with the impact of a strange environment. The difficulty must be remedied quickly to prevent ongoing anxiety attacks. There are several approaches you can use to help your relative overcome his or her anxiety.

1. There are effective medications that serve as antianxiety agents. A psychiatric consultation will result in a prescription. Your regular medical doctor is also able to provide the prescription.

2. People having anxiety, suffering distressing physical symptoms, worry unduly about their health. They frequently think

Making the Decision | 55

they are dying. Reassure your relative that anxiety does not cause death. Add that what is happening is as bad as it will get. You can say this with confidence as the nervous system memorizes a pattern. Each attack produces the same symptoms. They are awful, but they will not get worse. If not helped, your relative will have more attacks, but the intensity and format will not substantially change.

3. Reassurance is a good technique. Reassurance is not given in the form of dismissing the problem, but is an acknowledgment of the problem while pointing out that the anxiety always goes away and it will again. Give your relative credit for having the power to dispel the anxiety. The more he or she feels it will not harm him or her the more he or she will relax, and the sooner the anxiety will disappear. Your relative will feel in control.

4. Distract your relative. Get him or her to talk to you, to engage in an activity, hold him or her. When he or she orients to other people, physical contact, or an event, his or her mind is off the self and the anxiety diminishes.

5. If your relative knows how to practice progressive relaxation, encourage him or her to do it. If he or she does not know how, maybe you can learn together. Human beings cannot be relaxed and tense at the same time.

6. If your relative can be physically active, start walking with him or her. This burns off the excess adrenaline manufactured when in an anxious state. Bending, stretching, clapping, throwing a ball, are good exercises too.

Physical Symptoms

The stress of adjustment can result in physical symptoms. Two common physical problems seen during the adjustment period are insomnia and fatigue.

It is hard to sleep in a new bed, with the lights on, with a roommate who snores, and full of apprehension about what will happen next. Complaints about sleeping problems are common when in an unfamiliar environment. If your relative is situated near the nursing station it may be too noisy. If the roommate is disruptive the complaint is legitimate. Help your relative fix what can be fixed. Generally show concern and realize that the sleeping complaints will be tempered with time.

Fatigue that cannot be overcome with rest is typical of people in stress. The best way to help your relative dispel chronic tiredness is to help him or her make the home his or her home. Do not urge her or him to take it easy, but promote getting involved. Naturally, your relative will need ordinary amounts of rest, but he or she also needs something that interests him or her, some feeling of knowing what is happening around him or her, a familiarity with the people and protocol, and a sense of predictability in the environment so he or she does not have to be always prepared, on guard, or learning new procedures.

Family Adjustment

You must take care of yourself if you are to take care of your relative. You cannot be of much use to your relative unless you are of use to yourself. The process of caring for yourself consists of three steps:

1. Recognize your feelings.
2. Accept your feelings.
3. Work through, around, and with your feelings.

Recognize Your Feelings

In the last section the residents' adjustment was discussed. It was noted that there are expected emotional and physical reactions to stress. You were given suggestions on how to help your relative through that difficult period. It is as crucial to help yourself. You are also under stress and may have all or some of the same symptoms. Recognize them. Denial is not a good defense mechanism because life has changed and relationships have altered. They will never be the same. Your relative may expect more from you. Maybe you will be required to give less. Whatever happens, it will be different. Different means that something that was, is not. There is loss. With loss there is grief. Grief is the normal reaction to losing what was. Going through grief gets you ready for that which is to be. As you mourn what is no more you are giving up what you cannot have and preparing to invest yourself in what will come.

Grief is not the same for everyone. Some grief is of short duration. Some is protracted. Grief is a group of feelings that may include anger, guilt, depression, despair, withdrawal, fear, hopelessness, loneliness, anxiety, irritability, apathy, inability to concentrate, and disinterest. Not everyone will feel all these emotions and behaviors.

Grief can be the result of role reversal. The persons who made decisions, who were the caregivers, who showed an interest, are no longer the same when they go to a nursing home. An era is lost.

Guilt is part of grief. Guilt is the recognition that nothing is the same and that you have been part of the change. In the throes of grief it is usual to question if you did the right thing at the right time in the right way. Should you have done differently? On purpose, or unintentionally, others may contribute to your grief and guilt. The nursing home resident may question why he or she has to be in a nursing home, beg to go home, show anger, question your motives, or threaten you with withdrawal of love. Other relatives may suggest that your decision to assist with the nursing home placement was motivated by selfishness, meanness, or money. All this intensifies the grief/guilt syndrome. You probably are also tormenting yourself with doubts.

Recognize that these troublesome, painful feelings are normal throughout the adjustment period. Accept them.

Accept Your Feelings

You may as well accept your feelings. They are there. They are real. They are normal. Grief is a healing process. It must be accepted. Then energy can go into recovery. If the feelings are denied, all the energy goes into maintaining that fiction. Grief and guilt are fatiguing enough without further depleting your strength by pretending that negative emotions are not involved. If you do not accept your emotions you and your criticizing relatives will conspire to let you know that your misery is deserved. You need to know that your discomfort comes from loss and changes, not from being a bad person. Although the loss is permanent, your woe need not be. If you recognize and accept your feelings you can work them through without letting your relative take advantage of your vulnerability. Grief and guilt can lead to compensating behavior that does not help you, your relative, or the situation. For example:

Ms O missed her mother. The mother had lived with her, answered her telephone, cleaned, cooked, and gone with her on recreational outings. They had a good relationship. When Ms O's mother's Parkinson's disease made her unsteady on her feet, dependent in some activities of daily living, and unpredictably moody, Ms O knew her mother needed more care than she could give. She and her mother went nursing home hunting and found one that appealed to them more than the others. When Ms O's brother heard that the plans had led to admission he insisted that that was no way to treat their mother. When mother was found crying because she was homesick, Ms O buckled under and took mother home. She hired sitters. When that did not work out well she took a leave of absence from her work. She appealed to her brother for help. The brother said he had too many other responsibilities, but was glad Ms O was doing the right thing.

Ms O was not doing the right thing. She was acting out of grief and guilt. She harked back to what she had lost as she had missed her mother. She was overcome with guilt when her brother made his accusation; she was not sure that she was not being selfish and inconsiderate. When she saw her mother in tears she became sure that she had done something horrible. She forgot that her mother had agreed to the plan. She failed to recognize that her brother was not involved in her mother's care. She neglected to think through the matter of her mother's need for supervision and safety. She became woefully altruistic and decided that her mother was worth any sacrifice. Taking her home resulted in Ms O dropping out of her career, caused her mother to become more dependent and demanding, and culminated in mutual resentment and acrimony. The feelings could have been handled. They could have suffered through the loss. They could have remained friends.

Work Through, Around, and with Your Feelings

Come to terms with family conflicts. Nursing home placement of a relative puts added stress on a family that is already in trouble. The one who assists in the nursing home placement does not want to be the family scapegoat. It is an easy role to pin on a family member who already feels grief and guilt. However, if the family members know when they are vulnerable, they can take care of the emotions and be impervious to the assaults by uncharitable relatives. This means that the family problems have to be seen as long-standing distresses that can be put in perspective as the conflict that was there before placement and will remain a conflict during and after placement. The relatives responsible for the placement have to realize that the problem is a family problem, not a placement problem. It is not their fault. Their actions were sensible and thought out. The reasons need to be remembered, and any new decisions that are based on emotions resisted. When you're right, you're right.

The loss of the breadwinner, decision maker, matriarch, financial adviser, leads to double grief when that person is also the parent, the spouse, or a sibling. Can the roles be continued from the nursing home? Is the resident too debilitated to perform as in the past? Who takes on the roles? The family equilibrium is thrown off balance. Grieve and grow. Realize that the good memories cannot be taken from you, but the person that was is no longer. Your roles change as your responsibilities encompass those that used to be those of the resident. Do not be alarmed at resistance and resentment. Just know what you now have to do. Try to accept your enlarged role graciously and with confidence.

Decisions may have to be worked through again and again. Only when you are sure you did the right thing will you be able to be clear and consistent with your relative.

Sometimes it helps to talk to other people who can be objective, such as social workers and counselors, to assist you in looking rationally at what was done. Sometimes it helps to talk to others who have been through or are going through the same ordeal. Talk with the relatives of other residents. They will understand and be supportive.

Make a list of the events that occurred that led to nursing home placement. How did you feel and act? What did your relative do? Carry the list with you so you can refer to it when you are filled with doubts. You can be most effective when you accept the realities and work within the limitations. Everybody has a limit on what he or she can do. Recognize your limits and do what you can without guilt.

2
Residents' Rights

Nursing home residents have rights guaranteed them by federal law. At the time of admission the admissions coordinator will go over these rights with you and your relative, have your relative, or you if you are the responsible party, sign an acknowledgment that the Residents' Rights have been explained, that you were encouraged to ask questions, and that your relative was given a copy of the document.

Residents' Rights are the rights to which all United States citizens are entitled. The residents are not incarcerated and have not lost any of their inalienable rights. A truncated version of the rights follows.

1. Access to information about the facility and to personal medical records
2. Freedom to make decisions
3. Guarantees of confidentiality
4. Respect for privacy
5. A grievance procedure
6. Participation in activities of choice
7. Visits at personal convenience
8. Freedom of uncensored communication
9. Procedural safeguards on admission, transfer, and discharge

Residents' Rights, also known as Patients' Rights, is such an important document that this chapter will be devoted to the subject.

People living in nursing homes tend to abdicate their rights and at the same time give up personal power, self-respect and self-esteem. When they do this they lose a sense of themselves as responsible people whose lives have meaning. Thus, it is wise for you to know the Residents' Rights law and remind your relative of it at appropriate times. You will be emphasizing choice, responsibility, self-respect and dignity. Studies of these issues have shown that the more residents are assertive and make choices, the better they feel about themselves and the longer they live.

CHOICE

Choice is mentioned many times throughout the law. Residents are guaranteed choice by law. This does not mean that they are given what you or the nursing home staff think is good for them. They are to choose on their own.

Residents have the right to refuse medical treatment, no matter what anyone else thinks is best for them. They may be asked to sign a statement that treatment was refused so the nursing home staff can verify that the treatment was offered and recommended, but that the resident's choice was honored.

Residents have a right to choose their own personal physician. This means that the residents do not have to accept the doctor who provides services at the facility. They make their own selection and have ready access to the physician's name and telephone number so they may have a private conversation with their medical adviser whenever they want. All residents must have a physician because a nursing home is a medical facility and medical orders are required before a resident can live there.

Residents may choose to have living wills. They may choose someone to act on their behalf to carry out their wishes through guardianship or a durable power of attorney. A nursing home employee cannot be appointed to these positions.

Residents may choose to administer their own medication unless this is determined to be unsafe.

If you and your relative adhere to the Residents' Rights you will see that the residents are more important than procedures. This is a critical distinction because procedures can easily take ascendancy in an institution. You want to guard against that happening by helping your relative and the staff members look first to the needs of the person.

Residents can choose whether or not they want to contribute to the welfare and the running of the nursing home. If there is an appropriate volunteer job they will be welcomed into it. However, they are free to choose not to participate.

Residents may choose to have visitors at any reasonable hour. The nursing home staff cannot keep you from visiting at an off hour unless you are disruptive and put the residents at risk. If you can visit at times convenient for everyone it is better, but not necessary. Early to midmorning hours are the most difficult for receiving visitors because the staff are busy with baths, grooming, medication, and room readiness. If you want to see nursing staff as well as your relative, find out what times during the day they have a breather.

RESPONSIBILITY

The Residents' Rights law includes items that enhance residents' responsibility.

Residents have the right and responsibility to voice grievances. They are guaranteed this right without having to worry about reprisal. The grievance can be reported to the designated in-house ombudsman or to the social worker, director of nurses, administrator, or assistant administrator. If reporting to one of the above does not satisfy you or your relative, go to another one. If you are still not satisfied, you can contact the state long-term-care ombudsman (the telephone number should be publicly posted in the nursing home), file a civil rights or section 504 grievance, complain to the United States Department of Health and Human Services, or, if the nursing home is part of a chain, contact the regional or home office.

Your grievances or complaints within the facility are to be taken seriously. You can expect a reply from the staff within five days.

Residents have the right to be fully informed regarding their health status. Without this knowledge they cannot be responsible for making decisions that influence the course of their treatment and their lives.

Residents' Rights | 63

Residents have the right to be responsible for their own financial affairs unless a responsible party is designated. If your relative has always handled his or her own money, is alert and oriented, he or she may want to continue to do so. This gives people the feeling that they are in charge of their lives. Bear in mind that if he or she regularly mismanaged money, this will continue. People have the right to gamble, buy lavish gifts, blow their savings on clothes instead of needed false teeth, and smoke instead of pay for their laundry. As long as the board and room are paid the money is discretionary. You and the nursing home staff may not approve of the expenditures, but nursing home residents have as much right as anyone else to spend their money in the way they want, make mistakes, and run short of cash.

Nursing homes operate a patient trust fund system for the residents' convenience. This functions much like a bank. The residents can withdraw money during working hours. Residents can request to see their account balance.

Residents have the right to be part of the care-plan process. They have the responsibility for identifying problems, setting goals, and determining approaches on their own behalf. Residents' relatives are also to be notified and invited to the care-plan meeting, which is held once every three months for every resident in the facility. This is your opportunity to talk with the care team and have your relative's needs and problems addressed. These meetings are of consequence to you and your relative. This is when the team decides on the best plan of care to follow for the next ninety days.

The resident is to be included. He or she is then taking responsibility for his or her own welfare, goals, and care. This is a time for you and your relative to express what you want, when, and how.

People feel more responsible when they map their own day-to-day plan.

Some of the areas you and your relative may want to address during care-planning are

1. Participation in activities
2. Special interests
3. Rehabilitation plan
4. Roommates

5. Room location
6. Schedule of care
7. Food preferences and special diets
8. Weight gain or loss
9. Self-care
10. Any health problems
11. Discharge planning
12. Emotional concerns
13. Material needs
14. Behavior problems
15. Family issues
16. Volunteering
17. Visitors

The care-plan meeting is also a time to let nursing home staff know what the resident was like prior to nursing home admission. It is easy for staff members to judge the residents by what they see. They do not know about former interests, accomplishments, attitudes, preferences, and behaviors. With added information a more successful plan of care can be developed based on enhanced knowledge of what makes the residents who they are.

Each new resident is assessed and a Minimum Data Set (MDS) completed by the care team. This is updated regularly. It is this summary of information that helps the staff develop an effective and individualized care plan for that resident. This updating of your relative's status will assist you too. You will be able to determine progress or deterioration and problem areas. It is an extensive evaluation that covers

- Identification and background information
- Customary routine
- Thinking patterns
- Communication/hearing patterns
- Vision patterns
- Physical function
- Continence in last fourteen days
- Psychosocial well-being
- Mood and behavior patterns
- Activity pursuit patterns
- Disease diagnosis
- Health conditions
- Oral/nutritional status

- Oral/dental status
- Skin condition
- Medication use
- Special treatment and procedures

All these areas can and will be covered during each quarterly care-planning session.

SELF-RESPECT

When people feel good about themselves they feel better about others. Use the Residents' Rights regulations to improve your relative's self-respect. Some of the articles in the decree enforce rights and enhance self-esteem.

Residents have the right to privacy and confidentiality. You should observe this just as the staff must. There is not much privacy or confidentiality in group living, shared bathrooms, and personal care needs. Because of this, it is all the more necessary to respect personal privacy and information. All residents should have a private place available for visits with friends and relatives unless it is medically ordered that the resident be under constant medical supervision. Privacy for married couples is essential. Residents must be shielded from public view during bathing, toileting, and grooming activities. To this end they must be fully and decorously clothed when in the hallways and public rooms.

Staff members are required to knock or announce their presence when entering a resident's room. The room is treated like the resident's dwelling. Permission is needed to enter unless there are extenuating medical concerns.

All nursing home staff members are bound by confidentiality laws. They do not release medical information without the resident's or the responsible party's signature, unless the residents are being transferred to another medical facility. They do not tell one resident about another. They do not report circumstances of the residents' lives to anyone in the community. Information given the social worker during confidential counseling sessions need not be shared unless it affects the total plan of care. For example, the social worker does not have to reveal to other staff members a family skeleton or emotional concern from the past. The social worker will have to share information if the residents are planning suicide, threaten harm to another resident, or report that their family members are bringing them candy, sodas, and rich desserts when they are diabetic. Behaviors that are harmful to themselves or others cannot be kept confidential from care-team members.

Some of what people are is reflected in their choice of attire and in their personal possessions. It helps the residents feel good about themselves when they have some items with them that display their taste, are admired by others, or conjure up happy memories. In the same vein it makes for an all-around good feeling and brightens the day when the residents' clothes are complimented. Personal possessions are significant self-respect promoters. Residents have a right to retain and use their personal belongings as long as they do so in the space provided. They do not have the right to infringe on their roommate's side of the room and use up storage space beyond that assigned to them. Nor can possessions be dangerous or inappropriate or interfere with the comfort of the other residents. They cannot keep a handgun, blast their roommates out of the room with loudspeakers on their stereo equipment, or insist on keeping garlic in their bedside stand. Residents' Rights go only so far. One resident's rights cannot infringe on the rights of another.

Residents who are treated with courtesy and consideration feel self-respect. It is their right to be given adequate notice of discharge and room and roommate changes, except in instances of emergency. If your relative needs to go to a hospital, he or she will be taken as medically necessary. If your relative is physically abusing a roommate he or she will be moved within twenty-four hours' notice in response to an emergency situation. At such times you will be told of the events after the changes, but as soon as you can be contacted or within twenty-four hours. Since such things happen, it is imperative that nursing home staff know where and how to reach you. Check every three months to make sure your telephone numbers and whereabouts are current. Charts get reviewed and thinned out. Your present location may be inadvertently discarded and an old address kept.

It is not helpful for residents to be protected by withholding information. They have the right to know when rooms or roommates are to be changed so they can voice their objections, clarify their concerns, ask their questions, and prepare themselves for the event. Well-meaning but wrong-acting people think that what the residents do not know will not hurt them. It hurts self-respect to be manipulated, to be made to understand that one is not strong enough to know the truth, to see indications that one cannot be trusted with information, and to be treated as a piece of interchangeable room furniture rather than as a living, feeling human being.

Oftentimes staff people are protecting themselves rather than the residents. Notice is not given and the facts are evaded because unpleasantness is unwanted. They do not want to see the residents upset or hear their protests and accusations. It is rationalized that not telling them is to keep them from becoming distressed. In actuality, the staff members do not want to upset themselves. Everyone needs preparation time. That does not say that everyone needs time to learn to like what is happening. The residents may not be happy about a change, but they can get themselves ready for it. They feel some control if allowed to do part of the planning and manage certain parts of the move. They feel totally impotent if changes are made in what seems a haphazard, unplanned, and arbitrary way. Self-respect is doomed. Helplessness moves to the forefront. It should not be forgotten that residents can take responsibility for their attitudes and actions if they are given adequate notice as required by law.

DIGNITY AND RESPECT

The Residents' Rights edict states that all nursing home occupants will be treated with dignity and respect. Included in this category are safeguards against harsh and abusive treatment, freedom to congregate and organize in groups, freedom of speech, and specific amenities such as a safe, clean, comfortable environment. These are quality-of-life issues.

No Harsh or Abusive Treatment

Residents must never be physically abused. All unexplained breaks, bruises, scratches, or resident complaints of harsh treatment are reasons for a report to adult protective services. There is an abuse telephone line for adult and child abuse reporting in your telephone book listed under your state agency for health, welfare, and economic services. Any reports to this organization have to be investigated within twenty-four hours. Do keep in mind that the elderly nursing home resident may fall, run into objects, or have fragile skin bruised or broken during ordinary activities, while personal care is given, or, if agitated, by striking out or struggling with the caregivers at unpredictable times for inexplicable reasons. If you know this about your relative, discuss your observations and concerns with the charge nurse or the director of nurses. Only after you have fully explored the problem and understand it can you decide if it is a case of abuse or a sad and difficult fact of life that is related to your relative's temperament, behavior, and physical status.

Physical abuse can be seen. Verbal and emotional abuse is more subtle. It can be laughing at the residents, or mimicking or teasing them in a taunting or malicious way. Losing patience and speaking sharply to the resident who has asked the same question for the twelfth time is verbally abusive. It is easy to slip into another's distinctive manner of speech, to tease, and to feel irritation at repetitious statements and questions. As tough as it is to maintain an even disposition while caring for residents with vexing habits and offensive behavior, it must be done. Not everyone can do it, but it is the expectation that only those who can will be hired to care for residents in long-term-care facilities.

Having to wait too long to have the call light answered is neglect. Having to wait interminably to be helped out of bed, into bed, or left to sit in wet clothing is neglect. Nonetheless, residents will have to wait their turn. Not everyone can be first. The residents can state their time preferences, but the staff has to work out the schedule that takes into consideration medical priorities as well as preferences. Who gets what attention when hinges on who is on duty, what has to be done when, and whether or not there are emergencies. If immediate help is needed it should be provided, but the residents cannot be the ones to dictate the order and time of care. This is the responsibility of the head nurse. The residents have the right to know the approximate time that routine, scheduled procedures will take place. They should not spend the day waiting and wondering about their bath, their hair-care appointment, or when their snack will arrive. If this is not managed in an orderly fashion, too much time and energy go into worrying about care and too little into living a good life.

Staff members are not allowed to abuse residents. Residents are not allowed to abuse others, either. If a resident is dangerous to any of the occupants of the facility he or she can be asked to leave. And, as is the law in this country, prejudice is not allowed. Staff are not permitted to favor one nationality or religious or ethnic group over another. Residents may pick those they choose as friends and associates, but certain people cannot be kept from the common rooms or activities because of discrimination against them. Nursing homes employ and admit people of all races, religions, and nationalities. If your relative is offensive in his or her remarks or physically abusive he or she will be the one who is removed, not the people he or she finds objectionable.

Physical and chemical restraints are not necessarily instruments of abuse and are occasionally prescribed for medical reasons. They are to be used only as part of the care plan and under doctor's orders. They are not to be used for purposes of discipline ("Behave or I'll tie you up!") or convenience ("We don't have time to watch her, so make sure she stays in one place."). The residents have a right to be free of restraints used for these reasons.

Physical restraints most often seen in nursing homes are vest or waist restraints called poseys. These are used to tie residents to chairs or beds so they will not fall, slip, or hurt themselves. Agitated residents may climb over bed rails, fall out of bed, or pace to such an extent that they physically deplete themselves. Some residents have difficulty sitting up and need a vest posey to keep from sliding out of their chairs. Residents who pick at themselves, remove bandages, and pull out tubes may be prevented from doing so with wrist restraints. A gerichair may be a helpful protective device as it keeps residents from sliding out of the chair, but it is a restraint as residents cannot get out of them, nor can they move them as they can a wheelchair. Bed rails are helpful to keep residents from falling out, but they are restraints.

When restraints are used properly and where necessary they do help medically and may lead to more independence. Mrs. P felt insecure without her waist restraint to anchor her in her wheelchair. Mr. Q was afraid to go to sleep unless his bed rails were up. Ms S needed the support a gerichair offered. Without it she was unable to sit up or get out of her room.

Physical restraints cannot be used as wanted, only as needed, and only as prescribed by a physician for a medical reason, and then for specified and limited times. Restraints must be removed every two hours and the residents exercised. If bedridden, residents are to be turned every two hours.

Less restrictive physical restraints that may be effective are pillows, pads, and removable lap trays. Lower beds can be used instead of bed rails. Preventive approaches, such as anticipating needs for toileting, eating, or drinking, may avert agitation and precipitous actions that lead to falls.

Antidepressants, major and minor tranquilizers, and antianxiety medications are necessary for residents who have been evaluated and diagnosed as having certain psychological conditions. The psychoactive drugs help make life happier, saner, and easier for psychotic, anxious, angry, and agitated residents. Medication can moderate those conditions to the point that residents can function in a group setting, relate to others, and enjoy aspects of their lives. When medication is used for a good reason with good results there is no cause for alarm. If there is not an acceptable reason and the results are questionable it is considered a chemical restraint and it is against the law. If your relatives look and act drugged check out their medications and discuss them with the nurse and the doctor. There may be other ways to curb emotional and behavior problems, such as eye-hand coordination activities, exercise, and releasing anger through talking or physical movement. Eye-hand coordination projects require concentration. When the mind is occupied in this way it cannot also be preoccupied with thoughts of distrust and despair. Exercise drains off the adrenaline. Talk externalizes the problems.

Freedom to Meet

Residents have the right of association. They can meet to discuss anything they like for any reason. Well-meaning nursing home employees have prevented groups of residents from getting together because certain of them were considered to be troublemakers and others were regarded as cliquish. People have a right to grumble and a right to meet with others they enjoy. One is called freedom of speech. The other is called friendship.

Nursing homes have established groups for residents and their families. The residents' group is called the Resident Council. The family group is called the Family Council or Family Support Group.

Resident Council

The Resident Council is encouraged in long-term-care facilities as a vehicle to give residents a say in their own care and the running of the institution in which they live. It is rehabilitative to have an effective voice in self-government. The Resident Council is an established instrument for hearing, evaluating, and reporting complaints. It gives the residents responsibility for their own well-being and is a way to enforce residents' rights.

Resident Councils meet on a regular basis, usually once or twice a month, but can meet as often as needed or wanted. The officers of the Resident Council are the residents. They can assemble without a staff member present, but may request any staff member they want to appear. Usually one staff member is appointed to be the adviser. The Resident Council hears and investigates dissatisfactions. They instruct residents on safety and fire regulations. They give administration feedback on the quality of the services. They improve living conditions. Most of all, they protect the residents' interests. They cannot make decisions for professional staff, but they can influence nursing home policies and procedures.

All residents should support the Resident Council in any way they can. Some may be able to use the group only for complaints. Others will be able to attend meetings. Still others will provide leadership.

Resident Councils are run by and for the residents. They need to guard their autonomy. Staff members may move too fast or take action to solve problems in the way they think is right. This is not appropriate. Residents need to move at their own pace and determine their course in the way they want, not the way someone thinks they should.

Family Council

If the nursing home your relative lives in does not have a Family Council, talk to the social worker about organizing one or start it yourself. You have the guaranteed right to meet with other family members or residents.

A Family Council is established for the family members' benefit. It provides an opportunity to talk about feelings, worries, and concerns with people having similar experiences.

Family Councils are self-governed with officers elected from among the interested parties. A staff member, usually the social worker, serves as the adviser.

Since Family Councils are formed to meet the needs of residents' families they can be anything the families want them to be. Discussions of common problems provide a great outlet for distressing events surrounding nursing home placement and adjustment. The council can also be used for dialogue with staff, learning about aging, hearing of the facility's services, getting information on disease processes and self-help aids, socializing, and keeping up to date on federal, state, and local regulations that affect nursing home operations. They can be used to encourage, recognize, and praise effective staff contributions. Staff will be pleased and will respond to the support by continuing to do good work.

Freedom of Speech

Freedom of speech does not mean that you and your relative have the right to be verbally abusive to residents and staff. With rights come responsibilities. The same is expected of you and your relative as is required of staff and other residents. Do not lie, demean, or make threats. Be courteous, firm, and expect that problems can be solved.

You and your relative have a right to talk about concerns. Involve yourself in resolving small annoyances. The tendency is to hope it will not happen again, or that it will right itself. There is a fine line between being a complainer and an advocate. Just remember that small irritations, constantly repeated, can become an issue of great moment. If the vexations are happening to others, too, you or your relative may want to present it to the Resident Council or the Family Council. Freedom of speech means that you and your relative can say what you want. If you want to be effective you will pick your time and place and decide how you say it.

Residents have a right to talk about the subjects that interest them and have significance to them. One of these topics may be death. They have a right to prepare for their own death by talking about their fears of helplessness, pain, and being left alone. They may want to make plans for their possessions and their final arrangements. They may want to settle old scores or make amends. There may be some last words of advice or caring. Death is not a popular subject in this culture. Most people get the message that it is not a topic for conversation. Some people think that if they talk about it it sounds as though they are encouraging or accepting the idea. This is not the case. Indeed, death is a subject that deeply concerns the residents, and they should be given the chance to talk about it. Although some people stay mum on the matter to their dying day, others are vitally interested in making their wishes known and in taking as much control as they can. Thus, they need to be afforded the occasion to put their feelings, plans, and troubled thoughts into words. Staff and relatives are helpful when they can listen without changing the subject, quickly reassuring the residents that things will be all right, or telling them that they should not worry. The statement by elderly nursing home residents that they are ready to die, or wish they would die, is not a statement of suicidal intent, but an acknowledgment that they are ready to let go, that it is time, and that the life that had meaning for them is past and they are unwilling to reinvest in this phase of their lives. It is a passive acceptance that what will be, will be. As they adjust to nursing home living some residents will lose this feeling. Others will feel themselves in a holding pattern while they wait for the inevitable. Even though you may be uncomfortable with such statements, the residents have a right to talk about what is on their minds. They have a right to say what is preoccupying them. You and the staff have an obligation to listen.

Quality of Life

The residents' quality of life is enhanced by a safe, clean, comfortable environment. But the quality of life is best augmented if that life is not too safe or too comfortable. Residents are adults, not children. They can take their own risks and make their own decisions. They are accorded respect for their experience and judgment. Hence, safety must not be restrictive and comfort should not be smothering. Protection can paralyze. Institutionalized helplessness can result. This leads to decreased motivation and depression. Instead, residents need to feel in control of their environment. This can be done by enforcing residents' rights and allowing choices. This freedom of choice is so important to mental and physical health that choices should be made by the residents even if those choices may constitute a hazard. Remember that choice is guaranteed in the Residents' Rights law. The Residents' Rights document does not add the clause that the choice has to be in the residents' best interests as defined by family and medical staff. Choice is for the residents to make, according to their own inclinations.

Quality of life issues are involved in where the residents sit in the dining room, where the residents' belongings are placed in their rooms, and if their call bell is conveniently located and quickly answered. They should have their fears and concerns addressed, not fluffed off. If a resident complains about a stomach ache, the complaint should be taken seriously and acted on.

The state licensing and certification office inspects each nursing home each year to see if it is meeting specific standards. The facility must abide by these rules and regulations if it is to keep its license to operate. Quality of life matters are part of the licensing and relicensing procedure. The results of these surveys are available to the public. That includes you. Nursing homes have the report posted in a place for public viewing. If you don't see it, ask.

Residents' Rights Dilemmas

Rights for residents is a simple concept, based on values that United States citizens have embraced. Enforcing them in a nursing home is not so simple. The fact that they are spelled out for residents of long-term-care facilities is an indication of the complexities. Knowing some of the nursing home staff's quandaries in regard to this may be helpful to you.

1. Many nursing home residents are disoriented and have thinking impairments. Although they can make uncomplicated choices, indicate their needs, and have preferences, other choices may be beyond their comprehension. Their judgment and perceptions are faulty. They cannot sort through an array of facts to make an informed choice. They may feel threatened or at risk if urged to make a decision. They may be overwhelmed and become agitated if faced with many choices. Do the staff offer the right of choice in areas where they are capable and not give them this right in more difficult matters? Staff members need to know the residents well enough to make sure they exert all the rights they can, but do not force them into examining what they cannot understand. This is where family members can help. Concerned families know the residents' values better than do staff members. They can help the residents make choices based on what they think the relatives would want. This gives family members an opportunity to advocate on the part of the residents.

Residents are guaranteed confidentiality. Nursing home staff cannot keep critical information from involved relatives who are to be given twenty-four-hour notification of any changes in the residents' status. These rights conflict. Staff members share information freely with the families of disoriented residents. Many of these residents have not been declared incompetent. Nevertheless, their confidentiality is not strictly guarded. Nor should it be. Caring relatives need to know what is going on so they can be helpful.

Residents are to have privacy. Disoriented residents may need constant supervision, cannot be left alone because of potential danger, and would be confused, distracted, and frightened if staff members knocked on their doors and asked permission to enter. The nursing home would be responsible if the residents were in peril because they were allowed privacy.

2. The families and the residents may not agree. When the residents are alert, oriented, and know what they want, a conflict

can arise when the families' wishes are in opposition. The residents have a right to make their own decisions. The families may feel the residents' decisions are wrong, foolish, and precarious. They may hold the nursing home responsible if their relatives' decisions worsen their circumstances. Whose rights are protected? Do the nursing home staff members follow the residents' instructions or do they side with the families in overriding their wishes?

3. There is the ever-present fear of being sued. When are the staff members defending the residents' rights, being overprotective, or being neglectful? Caretakers have the responsibility to provide and protect. Does this include making sure the resident does not make decisions that go against family desires or medical advice? The staff is in the position of always having to make the legally and morally correct decision and being able to document sound reasons for doing so.

4. The nursing home staff have an obligation to protect every resident. Does looking out for the rights of one resident infringe on the rights of another? Whose rights are right?

5. The nursing home staff does not have total control over the delivery of medical services. Although residents are to be given all information regarding their health, the physician may refuse to discuss the medical facts with them. You and the staff may advocate a certain procedure and the medical doctor may not have the same point of view. What residents want and what is their right may not be available to them.

6. The residents may be passive in the face of medical authority. People are trained to accede to those in power. Medical settings tend to put people in the mind-set of following instead of taking responsibility. Residents will follow orders and choose what is indicated rather than work out independent decisions. This behavior perpetuates as paid staff feel they are doing their jobs if they do what they think is right based on their professional knowledge. Residents reinforce this by acknowledging their status by not questioning or disagreeing.

7. There is limited choice in some matters. Room assignment is arbitrary as there may be only one bed in one room available. Personal property choices are restricted by the small amount of

space at the residents' disposal and the fear that possessions will get lost, broken, or stolen.

Because Residents' Rights are so fragile and easily broken, it is all the more important to be totally clear on rights that can be enforced. To ensure residents' rights, nursing home staff must treat each resident as an individual, taking into consideration abilities, background, needs, values, and potential. You can help them understand these aspects of your relative.

3

Life after Placement

Life in a nursing home is not the end of life, but a part of the continuum of life. It is not good or bad, just different. As with many things, it is what you make it. It cannot be what was. It can be a new and rewarding experience. Ms S and Mr. T found stability, security, belonging, and each other in the nursing home and thought it was a fulfilling time in their lives. This may not be true for you and your relative. It may be only a tolerable time. But you can help in making it as good as it can be.

The nursing home resident is faced with making many adjustments. There is a new place to live, new procedures and schedules, different people; frequently there are health problems. You have to adjust to having a relative in a group setting, sharing with a team of health care experts, and seeing deterioration. Your first duty is to handle your own adjustment. Then you can help your relative get involved in nursing home life.

STAY INVOLVED

The residents in nursing homes who do not have families are considered people with special needs as they do not have the support and attention that residents with families have. This is just one indication of how valuable a family is to a resident.

Importance of Family

Families have special meaning. There is a shared history. These are people who have known the resident through good and bad times. They know what is liked and disliked. Communication can be in shorthand—long explanations are unnecessary. Families know the problems and accept each other anyway. Family members can still see the spouse as a young, vital, and alluring person and the parent as in charge and responsible.

No one else has the relationship a family has that has spent years living in the same household. It is a compliment to tell people they are like a mother or father or sister or brother to them. People get from their families their first ideas of who they are, of values, and of how to view the world.

Families know what contributions each has made. The emergence of early good feelings of self-esteem, security, and belonging comes from the family. The family is the first line of survival.

Only the family is competent to interpret the resident to the staff, to explain why he or she is the way he or she is. The family can help the staff members see the whole person, what the resident is besides old and frail.

Advocacy

Because relatives understand and know each other better than do people who have recently become the caregivers, relatives can best help the caregivers understand the relative's needs if the resident cannot make him- or herself understood.

Having an advocate, someone on one's side, gives the resident more security. He or she feels protected. He or she thinks the relatives will not let anything bad happen to him or her. Even if the resident does not have to use the relatives to defend him or her, he or she feels stronger because they are there. Having relatives is like having a good insurance policy or a good defense system. You can actively advocate for your relative by

1. Explaining relative's likes and dislikes
2. Monitoring health and treatments
3. Checking clothes and clothes care

4. Elaborating on medical history by pointing out what worked when similar problems happened in the past
5. Encouraging the resident to demand his or her rights and reporting infringements of residents' rights
6. Helping the relative get involved in day-to-day nursing home life.

Support

The best support families can give is the support of being there. Even if the relative cannot hear or talk, he or she can be aware of a supporting presence. This is comforting, meaningful, and supportive.

Being supportive is listening and trying to understand. You do not have to solve the problem, but you may want to try to get at what is disturbing your relative. You may ask, "What can I do?" "What do you want me to do?" They may only want an audience. What a luxury to be able to talk about a problem without getting advice on what you should do, or being told that what you did was wrong!

You do not have to have all the answers for your relative. You may just have to help with alternatives. Mrs. U was having problems with her roommate. She felt she had to move. Her daughter helped her look at some ways to work out the problem with her roommate or to get a new roommate in the room she was in. There was not just one way to handle the problem. There were choices. Mrs. U's daughter was supportive of whatever the resident decided.

Restorative

Families can enrich the resident's ability to cope because they are advocates and supportive and the resident can feel their strength. However, if the relatives are too protective and show alarming concern they may be killing the resident with kindness. If the relatives are solicitous to the point that the resident gets the message that he or she cannot do anything, then the relatives are the antithesis of restorative agents. The resident feels there must be something wrong with him or her if the relatives are that worried about her or him. The resident figures that he or she may as well give up and stop doing for her- or himself. Be caring, but not crippling. Be excited and happy for anything the resident can do.

See the Benefits

You want your relative to get the most out of nursing home care. To accomplish this, help her or him see the benefits. If your relative sees you admiring aspects of nursing home living he or she is more likely to see the good parts too. If it pleases you he or she will conclude that there is something pleasing about the place. Praise what you can so the resident can take pride in the surroundings. The nursing home is her or his home and he or she wants to feel good about it, wants to like being in a place that looks good and has a good reputation.

Some of the benefits you will want to point out to your relative are

1. Entertainment, parties, activities produced and designed and brought to the nursing home for the residents' convenience and enjoyment
2. Educated professionals to provide care and consultation
3. A well-balanced diet delivered through regular meals
4. Inspections, surveys, quality control, rules and regulations to make sure the residents are protected and cared for
5. Help with anything for which they need help
6. Clean, well-maintained surroundings
7. Opportunities for friendships
8. Chance for rehabilitation
9. Immediate attention in an emergency
10. Security

The Resident's New Life

Anybody who experiences a new lifestyle, such as entering school, getting married, having children, moving to a different area, is filled with thoughts of the experience. This is part of the adjustment, but is also part of day-to-day living. Nursing home events and reports on other residents may not be the most stimulating conversational topic to you, but it is your relative's life! You may feel distressed that the relative seems more interested in the new acquaintances and activities than in you. Because it is new and vital this is normal. This is also because nursing home residents do more than just reside in a nursing home. Nursing homes are set up to be the residents' entire life. It is more than room and board. It is intimate encounters with caregivers, home-delivered health, education, entertainment, welfare services, and constant contact with other human beings. Nursing home life is a world of its own. Residents do not have to leave the facility, much less their beds, to get everything they need. Their world gets pretty small. People who otherwise might not be a selected part of their experiences become important in the residents' lives. You may not share the interests. You may be bored with the seemingly minuscule observations of day-to-day life. You may be jealous that others appear to have more consequence in your relative's life than you do. Others may seem to take your place in his or her affections and priorities. Do not be put off by this. Even though the person who delivers the mail may be a chatty highlight to the resident's day, no one can replace family. Family members may feel unappreciated and taken for granted, but what else is new? If you cannot take a family member for granted now and then, one of the attributes of having a family is voided. Sure, love, understanding, and support from family is a precious commodity that needs tending, but the quality of stability and constancy is what makes it special. Do not feel that there can be a substitute for you, no matter how good or bad your relationship with your relative is, because this is not the case. Other relationships are different—helpful or unhelpful, fun or tedious, loving or stressful, but they are not family relationships.

You can remind your relative of the unique nature of your relationship by showing interest in mundane accounts of her or his everyday life. Not everyone will do that for him or her. Bring in regular bits of information from the outside that includes anecdotes about neighbors and relatives, making your relative a part of the world exterior to the nursing home. He or she may seem more interested in his or her reports than in yours. Give the report anyway. You are the link to the "real" world. Your relative will use these topics for conversations with others within the facility where he or she may bore residents and staff with stories about the family. Over all, be glad that your relative is integrating into group living and thinks you are interested in hearing the details of what is going on with him or her.

Game Playing

Long-standing relationships develop their own patterns of game playing. Arguments and disappointments degenerate rapidly into a codified procedure, with each playing the assigned part. Game playing connotes an unpleasant interchange with a dismal ending. Game playing is indicative of a troubled relationship that results in a loser and a winner. When the game playing is with your relative in a nursing home both you and the relative lose. Since the game involves two people, if one quits, the game is over. You can be the one to stop it. Do not let your buttons be pushed. Do not play the expected role. Stop knee-jerk reactions. Since the game was never fun you will not miss it. Your relative will have to find new ways to deal with you. Your relationship will change for the better.

Mrs. V cried whenever she saw her daughter. The daughter, overcome with guilt, would explain and apologize and feel miserable about her mother's nursing home placement. Visiting became a dreaded chore that reinforced her guilt. Then she changed. She changed by not succumbing to remorse; instead, she related cheery news from home, discussing community events, or not talking at all and waiting out the tears. Fairly often the daughter planned her visit around a nursing home activity they both attended. This prevented Mrs. V from using the time to elicit sympathy. When Mrs. V did not get the result she wanted, the behavior stopped.

Mr. W was given to the silent treatment. This generally reduced his son to begging for forgiveness for whatever he did or did not do. Mr. W would eventually relent, but his son was always worried he might say or do the wrong thing. One day the son told Mr. W that he had done the best he could, meant no harm, talked about family and friends, and left. After a few more visits with this tactic, Mr. W's manipulation stopped.

Mrs. X always told the nursing home staff how wonderful they were and she told her daughter how they neglected her. After several instances in which the daughter confronted the staff and the staff explained how well Mrs. X was doing, they figured out what was going on. The daughter decided to have Mrs. X accompany her when she discussed complaints with the staff. The complaints stopped.

Mr. Y was doing very well. He willingly participated in the restorative program, attended several activities, and made friends. He ate all his meals. When his wife arrived he explained that he felt terrible, was not getting better, couldn't eat, and the staff members were making him do too much. Mrs. Y was at war with the staff over her husband's care. Their visits were taken up with problems. A staff member cut through the issue by going over the resident's chart with Mr. and Mrs. Y after first obtaining Mr. Y's permission. Mrs. Y recognized what her husband was doing and concentrated on encouraging his successes. As she changed the rules of the game, he changed and played by the new rules, which included telling what he did instead of fabricating negative reports.

The procedure for stopping game playing is

1. Identify the game;
2. Decide not to play;
3. Change the rules.

Education on Aging

You will be better able to cope with your elderly relative if you educate yourself about physiological and psychological changes of aging. Much of what happens is because of aging and disease processes. These alterations in physical and mental health affect how the elderly function. If you understand what is going on you will be better able to accept and handle the changes, not take negative behaviors personally, and prepare yourself for what may happen next.

To get information, you can talk with the nurse, doctor, and social worker in the nursing home. They will be able to tell you more about your relative's specific condition and give you general information about the problem. Many diseases, such as cancer, lung, heart, Alzheimer's and Parkinson's, have national societies that supply educational material. There are support groups for relatives of people with Alzheimer's disease, strokes, and cancer, to name a few. The nursing home social worker can tell you which groups meet where. The library is a source for books and videos on arthritis, diabetes, and more. All these diseases have an emotional and physiological impact that cannot be ignored.

Besides the deterioration caused by disease there is the slow and steady erosion of the body. A quick look at the various systems follows.

Skin: The skin becomes less elastic, less durable. It wrinkles, bruises more easily, becomes dry, and develops spots. The skin is thinner, the veins more prominent.

Skeleton: The spinal column becomes shorter by about one and one-half inches. The bones become porous and brittle and break more easily. The joints are painful and stiff. The back becomes stooped, the neck more stiff and rigid. This thrusts the head and neck forward. The bones and hips bend and balance is poor.

Muscles: Muscles atrophy. There is decrease in strength, endurance, and agility.

Nervous System: There is a short-term memory loss, less sensitivity to hot and cold. There is shaking and loss of balance. There may be personality changes in which there is pessimism, possessiveness, loss of interest, and poor adaptability. Messages within the nervous system travel more slowly, increasing response time and slowing reflex reaction time.

Somatic System:

Sound: There is hearing loss. It is harder to hear high frequency tones or determine the direction from which the sound comes. Lower tones can be heard more readily when expressed at a slower pace.

Sight: There are decreased tears. Peripheral vision decreases. The pupils adjust slowly to light and dark. There is lessened ability to focus on close objects and discriminate fine details. There is more sensitivity to glare, less to color.

Touch: There is less responsiveness to pain, temperature, pressure. It is more difficult to gauge texture by touch.

Smell and Taste: Ability to smell decreases. There is loss of taste buds. Food tastes bland.

Respiratory System: The lungs are less efficient and have less reserve capacity and tolerance for exercise and stress. There is susceptibility to respiratory disease. There is a lessened ability to cough or deep breathe.

Digestive System: Saliva production is one third that of a younger person. Swallowing is more difficult. The gastric acids are weaker, the action in the intestines slower. There is constipation. Spicy food is tolerated less well.

Cardiovascular System: There is a lower maximum attainable heart rate. The heart must work harder to obtain less. It is hard to cope with stress as it takes a long time for the heart to return to a normal rate. There is poor circulation, less blood flow to the vital organs, and more likelihood of arrhythmias.

Urinary: The bladder capacity is reduced, leading to a frequent need to urinate. There is more urgency because of less acute bladder sensory receptors. There is a susceptibility to infections. Prostate problems are common.

Temperature Maintenance: Perspiration decreases. There is less ability to control and change body temperature to adapt to the surrounding temperature.

Remember that your relative is changing due to factors beyond his or her control. He or she compensates for these changes as he or she adjusts to the aspects of aging and to chronic disease conditions. But biological influences may well change your relative in ways neither of you anticipated.

In the resident's efforts to cope with health problems he or she may resort to methods that are deemed ineffective by the medical community. Medical staff may urge him or her to discontinue the practice. In spite of this medical attitude make it your business to help your relative continue to take vitamins, wear a copper bracelet, put vapor rub on his or her chest, eat chicken soup, or do any of the rituals that make the resident feel better. Much of healing is psychological. If your relative thinks it helps her or him, it probably does.

ACTIVITIES

Activities are a wide range of preferences, pursuits, programs, and projects. The larger the choice, the better the nursing home's activity department. Activities can mean spectator events, individual hobbies, group projects, educational presentations and classes, outings, passive or experiential involvement, group or individually tailored enterprises. Activities include both those that continue from the resident's prior living habits and those that are part of the organized nursing home program.

Community Activities

You are part of activities outside the facility. Nursing home residents want to get out if they are able. Some count the day as uneventful unless an external excursion is part of their experience.

Residents who do not go out are those with physical or mental problems that counterindicate being away from medical supervision.

Some residents are so physically disabled that they cannot be managed outside the facility. They cannot transfer from wheelchair to car unassisted. Most metropolitan areas have buses with wheelchair lifts, or a hoyer lift can be used for the transfer. With these complications outings are more difficult, but not impossible.

Residents can be too sick, too frail, too dependent in activities of daily living to manage away from their caregivers. However, a severely impaired stroke victim who was incontinent, could not eat without assistance, or walk, or talk, had a family that managed to have her at their home for a family reunion. It is not insurmountable, but oftentimes it is very hard.

Residents whose health is delicately balanced take a risk when they leave the nursing home and a strict medical regimen. They may eat wrong, rest less, get off schedule, and end up sicker, hospitalized, or dead. If you take such a person out it is best to limit the time away and then closely follow medical instructions. If results of the visit are potentially physically disastrous you may need to weigh the benefits of outings against the outcomes. As far as the resident is concerned the outing may be worth sickness, hospitalization, or even death. Some risks are worth anything.

Certain residents cannot leave the nursing home at all because their physical limitations and health status are so severe that they are in a position that allows no such option. Others may be able to manage with extensive help, but their relatives are unable to physically or emotionally provide such help. They may be unequipped by training or predilection.

Residents who are disoriented can be so confused, frightened, and agitated in unfamiliar surroundings that it is a disservice to put them through a situation that is beyond their coping skills. They may be able to manage it physically, but not emotionally. People with short-term memory problems do not appreciate or have the ability to contend with new experiences. If you must take your disoriented relative out, take her or him to places she or he remembers, with one or two people who are well known to her or him. If you want to take him or her to lunch or to a shopping mall, be planful. Always go to the same restaurant or home and leave the mall as soon as the stimulation appears excessive for your relative.

Disoriented residents may talk of leaving the facility, but a time away, however short, is often unwise because of their discomfort and fear. They have a distorted sense of time. Five minutes into an outing and they may be ready to return or move on because they think they have been away for ages. You will find such a short expedition frustrating, and you'll wonder why you bothered.

One of the more dismal situations concerns the resident whose relatives cannot take him or her from the facility because returning her or him is such a traumatic battle. Some relatives have found that they can take the residents out if they do not take him or her to a family home. A lunch at a restaurant or a ride works fine. Others have discovered that eliciting a promise of compliance with the plan is effective. Still others have sorrowfully learned that home visits are not workable.

Rides

Many residents like to go for rides. Their forays into the community are so infrequent that changes are always apparent and interesting. Visits to old haunts elicit the valuable and pleasant activity of reminiscing and life review.

If tolerated, a visit to your home is welcomed by the resident. This can be done routinely or offered as a special occasion. If residents are able to leave the facility with comparative ease and are in no medical or emotional jeopardy, visits outside obligatory holiday gatherings are in order.

Holidays

Holidays and special family occasions are crucial times for inclusion. The decision has to be made as to whether or not it is physically or mentally dangerous to encourage the relative's participation. The risk must be weighed against the benefits. If the relative is able to be at the family gathering, make sure that he or she is not ignored. Talk with her or him. Get younger members of the family to take time to speak to him or her. Seat your guest where he or she can be part of the festivities. Remember your relative in special ways, such as with food he or she likes, an appropriate present, words of kindness. Try to protect the relative from getting overly tired.

Friends

Visits to friends' homes are special events. It is interesting for the residents to be guests and to note that time has not stood still in their absence from the community. Many decorative items will have changed. At the same time they will experience the timeless sameness of the friendship and the friends' style of living. There are variety and security through what changes and what remains the same.

It is hoped that friends visit the resident in the nursing home, too. It is also hoped that you and the friend visit at the resident's convenience. The belief that nursing home residents have nothing to do and are delighted to receive visitors at any time is a fallacy. This is a misconception for three reasons.

1. Residents have a set schedule for personal care, eating, and therapies.

2. Residents have activities and special programs they want to attend. Bingo is the long-standing favorite. Just like everyone else, they have a time they rest and a time they watch their regular television programs.

3. Residents feel better about themselves when they feel better about their lives. They feel better about their lives when they

have some control. Being consulted about visiting times is welcomed and gives some of the needed control. Being done to and for is not a comfortable state. Having friends visit because they want to at a time opportune for both produces satisfying feelings.

Asking staff members about visiting times for your relative is not the most effective approach. They are as likely as anyone else to disregard the resident's wishes and say to come at any time. The reason for this is that they do not take time to consult with the individual resident and they are encouraged to allow visiting at any hour because of the Residents' Rights law. Make visiting plans with your relative just as you would when visiting a person in the person's own home.

Clubs

Whenever possible, membership in organizations, clubs, and societies should be continued even if all the resident gets out of it is the association's newsletter. There is still a sense of belonging to something (church group), supporting a cause (environmental group), or getting help (self-help group). If residents can attend the meetings, all the better. Generally, they will need transportation. Relatives can help by providing this. Some of the clubs meet in members' homes. The nursing home residents should be able to offer their home for meetings, too. Expect the facility to accommodate an occasional organization's get-together, providing space, and, if necessary, refreshments.

Interests

If the resident was involved with hobbies or collecting, help him or her keep up the interest through visits to stores, displays, or shows devoted to the objects of her or his interest.

Learning

Nursing home residents are learning continually, just as everyone else does. They also enjoy the opportunity to acquire knowledge and interesting facts presented in interesting ways. Do not forget that your relative lives in a nursing home, and the emphasis is on live. While he or she lives, the resident can learn and finds that just as exciting as you do. Take your relative to short presentations at the library, the community center, or the local college.

Entertainment

Accompany the family member to a play, an instrumental music program, or some form of entertainment he or she does not normally see in the nursing home. Spare her or him from boredom and lack of variety. If he or she does not have the stamina to sit through the entire presentation, recognize this and handle any resentment you may feel at having to leave early. Just be happy that your relative could enjoy part of the program. If it irritates you to see a portion of a movie, see it in its entirety when you can go alone. And do not expect gratitude or total enjoyment. Your relative may not approve of the language, the dress, or the plot. He or she has the right to be critical. That does not mean he or she did not enjoy the excursion.

Nursing Home Activities

Activities provided in nursing homes are more than entertaining. They are therapeutic in the sense that they ameliorate physical or mental problems. They can be designed to draw out the isolated person, cheer up the depressed person, orient the confused person, or get the immobile person to be more physically active. While the therapeutic effects are taking place the facility's activities are pleasurable, distracting, and fun.

Each resident's activity needs are included in the care plan and revised and updated quarterly. The plan of care contains

1. Ways to involve the residents in the nursing home community and help them adjust to group living.
2. Activities to prevent mental and physical deterioration through exercises that stimulate the mind and the body.
3. Methods for reducing agitation, depression, fear, anxiety, or any debilitating behavior or emotion.
4. A plan for compensating for limitations through special devices or alternative activities.
5. Measures for realizing meaningful participation and belonging.

Nursing home activity programs are expected to meet any special needs of any resident. The resident in a coma and the alert, oriented resident who is able and willing to participate are to have recreational prescriptions. You should be aware of this and share your knowledge of the resident and your ideas with the activity coordinator. These professionals want a successful program and want participation from your relative. Let them know what fascinated your relative in the past and what form of activities he or she pursued. Did the resident prefer solitary adventures, group participation, team sports, craft work, spectator events, culture, or sight-seeing? All these interests can be accommodated. Activities are offered for everyone in the facility—for specific groups, and for the individual. Seek out activities that will suit your relative and encourage him or her to attend, or attend with her or him. Know and respect your relative's activity schedule so you do not regularly interfere with the favorites.

Many activities are geared to enticing the residents out of their rooms, getting them to socialize, and distracting them from their day-to-day preoccupations with their problems. These activities include sing-alongs, film and slide shows, music programs, demonstrations, and various entertaining presentations. There may be food-oriented activities because refreshments are a big draw. Teas, popcorn parties, ice cream socials, international and favorite recipe dinners, and wine and cheese parties are popular.

Some activities for groups involve skill and provide the extra excitement of competition and rewards. Sports equipment is modified so that wheelchair contestants can participate and the frail elderly will not be hurt. For example, volley ball is played with a balloon rather than a regular ball. The shuffleboard court is shorter. The bowling is set up manually. The ball and pins are lightweight plastic. Darts, ring toss, and a putting golf game are also effective.

Bingo is probably the number-one activity in any nursing home. Games such as dominoes, chess, checkers, cards, and board games are offered, too.

Parties are for all residents. Birthdays are generally celebrated monthly with one party for everyone who had their special day that month. This does not preclude you from commemorating your relative's birthday on the correct date with family and friends in attendance, or throwing a bash for everybody. What you do to make your relative's birthday a special event is up to you. It may be attending the nursing home group party or it may involve a more personalized festivity.

Holidays promote conviviality through special decorations and appropriate merrymaking. You can expect that the nursing home will be seasonally decorated for New Year's, Presidents' Day, St. Patrick's Day, Easter, Mothers' Day, Fathers' Day, Memorial Day, Independence Day, Halloween, Thanksgiving, Christmas, and any other religious or cultural day that is special to many of the occupants of the home.

Religious services and bible classes are not considered activities, but are arranged through the activity department. Many residents enjoy them, but if they are able, prefer going out to their own houses of worship. Some churches provide transportation to the sanctuary for those who need it. If feasible, you will want to transport your relative to church.

Some activity groups are organized to give the residents feelings of accomplishment through tangible results from their efforts and abilities. These are the craft groups. The crafts are modified to accommodate people with less dexterity and with vision problems. They still end up with viable products. The crafts may include ceramics, jewelry making, dolls, clay, stuffed animals, mosaics, sewing, weaving. Along the same line is the gardening project. Some facilities have built off-the-ground plots that can be tended by wheelchair-bound residents. The gardeners get to eat the results of their labors or decorate their rooms with the flowers they grow.

Special groups are set up for residents with special needs. These are the reality-orientation groups; men's groups; discussion groups for the alert, oriented residents; and groups to recognize and guide residents who are volunteers.

Rehabilitative groups are organized to help residents with cognitive (thinking) impairments. There are exercise, remotivation, social-skill training, and self-esteem groups.

Self-help groups may include Alcoholics Anonymous, reminiscing, life review, and groups for learning and monitoring relaxation skills.

Learning groups are provided to exercise and stimulate minds and get the residents involved in life. These groups may be based on trivia, news and weather reports, political speakers, or health topics.

In-room activities include sensory stimulation (experiences to stimulate the senses such as items to touch or smell), jigsaw puzzles, talking books, pet visits, one-to-one conversations and therapies, and individualized exercise programs.

Individual activities that are separate but part of the group involve writing for the facility newsletter, working in the resident's store (gifts, sundries, and snacks sold by and for the residents), and participating in talent shows.

Outings are regularly scheduled and enjoyed by those who are able to go. There are trips out for lunch, to the zoo, museums, parades, the circus, fairs, plays, an ice show, or any other event. Nursing homes are frequently provided a block of free tickets for residents' use. A boat ride is popular, as is a picnic in the park. Because of the residents' diminished stamina and need for assistance these tours must be carefully planned and require extra help. Your volunteer aid will be appreciated if you are able to give it.

This is a smattering of what you can expect from the nursing home activity department. Besides arranging the activities, the department personnel must make sure that all the residents know of the events and have a way to get to them. There should be large posted activity schedules in each wing, smaller individual schedules in the possession of each resident, and regular announcements made on the facility speaker system. They have to give constant invitations and encouragement, but are not allowed to coerce any resident to attend anything.

A significant problem is getting the residents to the activities. People with short-term memory problems will not remember to go or may get lost on the way. Many residents will need assistance to get to the event and a promise that they will not be abandoned there, but helped back to their rooms. If you see activities poorly attended, look into the transportation procedure. There may be no organized effort to get the residents to the activity. The activity department employees cannot do it all on their own. They need volunteers and help from the nurses and the nursing assistants to gather up all those who will benefit from and enjoy the activity. If you notice that this is not a team effort, make a complaint. Your relative has a right to the help he or she needs to get to all the activities he or she may want to attend.

Companions

With a move to a nursing home people no longer need to be isolated, but have access to many acquaintances and friends. Residents find an affinity with roommates, other residents, staff members, and volunteers. A mutual enjoyment and caring develops.

At first blush, so many people in close quarters is overpowering. The tendency is to pull back and set personal boundaries. This is a normal and healthy reaction. It does not indicate that the new residents will not get involved. It indicates that they have to first get their bearings. If your relative continues a reluctance to venture out after the first one or two weeks, you will want to look for the reasons for this behavior. You cannot be all things to your relative. You want to share him or her with others. You want him or her to get all that can be gotten from nursing home living. One of the valuable assets in group living is the propinquity of other people your relative may enjoy. Some of the possible causes of isolation follow.

1. Maybe your relative has always been a private person and is struggling to maintain that stance among the throngs that now surround her or him. That is an understandable preference, but it does not have to continue that way. Remarkable as it may seem, people of any age are capable of changing behavior patterns to fit alterations in circumstances and in themselves. Given new living arrangements and easy accessibility to people and activities, the loner may develop an interest in other people and enjoy their company, or pick just one favorite chum. Do not decide that your relative will always be the way she or he was. Give her or him the chance to develop the social side. You can help by engaging roommates and staff members in conversations that include your relative. You can accompany the resident to some spectator events in the facility and to more casual gatherings such as food-related socials and parties.

2. Proximity is the reason most people make friends. They

meet people at work or in the neighborhood. The same is true in nursing homes. Residents are not all so mobile that they can take themselves out of their areas and down other halls in search of friends. They meet their roommates, their dining companions, and others in rooms near their own. If your relative complains that the roommate is incompatible, the dining companions are gross, and the nearby residents are unacceptable, look into the accusations. They may have foundation. If your relative cannot make the request, assist her or him in getting more amenable surroundings. If the resident is to make friends she or he will need more like-minded and equally able people around so she or he can have satisfying relationships.

3. It is possible that your relative is afraid of being around the many disoriented residents. Not only can these residents be irritating and disruptive, but certain people, already worried about their own declining abilities, are concerned that their deterioration will be accelerated if they associate with the mentally impaired. It helps to let your relative know that senility is not catching. It also helps if you get your relative out among other residents who also need alert, oriented individuals for congenial association. If the activity department does not offer activities for alert, oriented residents, suggest that they plan to do so on a regularly scheduled basis.

4. If your relative has personality problems that prevented him or her from making friends in the past he or she will take those problems with him or her to the nursing home. If he or she is shy, defensive, hostile, demanding, or difficult, he or she may be able to get help for the problem. The nursing home team can address the difficulties in the care plan. The staff social worker will devise a plan that will work toward helping your relative learn to get along with others while feeling better about him- or herself. You and your relative can discuss this privately with the social worker and attend the care-plan meeting.

5. If your relative is too sick to make friends there is not much you can do. Physical problems bring on weakness and pain, but special associations will be made with compassionate roommates, kind, careful, and caring staff members, and visits from residents who volunteer to visit room-bound nursing home occupants. Take note of the special quality of these relationships.

Also note that anxiety is lessened, along with pain, when a supportive human being is present and is a good listener.

6. You may be taking too much of the relative's time or your visits may be too erratic. If you visit every day, all day long, your relative's life is wrapped around yours. The resident does not have the opportunity to form other relationships. If you would like to see your relative become part of the nursing home community you will have to arrange your visits around his or her schedule. If you visit at unscheduled, irregular times, you will find your relative spends all the time waiting for your visit since he or she does not know when it will occur. This is very frustrating to nursing home staff because it is impossible to engage residents who are always too preoccupied. They refuse to go on outings, to activities, or have a conversation because they are always concerned that it will interfere with the expected family member's visit.

7. Some residents have friends, but do not want their relatives to know about it. They fear that the relative might be jealous or that the relative will feel unneeded and will visit less often. Your duty is to be part of your relative's life, not his or her entire life. Let the resident know you are happy he or she has made friends and that you will continue to be PART of his or her life, just as you have always been. People-sharing is healthy. A nursing home is the perfect setting for having a number of people involved with your relative in a number of different ways.

Personal relationships do develop and are meaningful to the residents. They find people they can confide in, people who offer them support and concern, and people they enjoy. Some male/female relationships turn into love, and marriages result. Family members have been known to object to romances, but when both residents are alert, oriented, and know what they want, the staff cannot prevent them from associating with whomever they want. It is the residents' right. You cannot stop it either, as you are not available for twenty-four-hour interference. If the relationship has positive meaning to your relative and he or she is capable of making choices, you may as well be happy that he or she is happy. If your relative needs protection from exploitation because of incompetence, make this clear to the nursing home administration. If they cannot provide protection you may want to consider a transfer. However, do not be too hasty. If your relative is disoriented in some areas of comprehension, but can take pleasure in the attentions of another person, the spark of special caring will enhance the resident's sense of well-being. One never gets too old for special relationships or enlivening flirtations.

It is definitely difficult to deal with disruptive, disoriented residents, but as your relative adjusts he or she will learn when to avoid and when to be helpful. Disoriented residents may wander into others' rooms, take what is not theirs, get hostile for no apparent reason, and repeat certain phases. This is hard to accept. The disoriented cannot be stopped from moving around the facility or from expressing themselves in their own way. The nursing home can set aside a wing for the more disoriented and provide closer supervision. Often the nursing staff tries to keep them situated around the nursing station or involved in activities that distract and entertain them.

Expect that your relative will experience a sense of loss when friends die or a staff member who was depended upon quits the job. Any change, such as remodeling, schedule adjustments, different therapies, is difficult. The more your relative is personally involved in the change the more difficult it will be. Do not diminish your relative's sense of loss. It is important to her or him. Help the resident get through the disruption and readjust to schedules and people. Give it time. Give your relative the opportunity to grieve and to make new friends.

4

Personal Possessions

The facility provides the residents with basic necessities. The room furniture and linens are supplied. Hospital gowns are available and may be preferred if the resident is bedridden and needs a great deal of care because of the severity of the physical problems, skin-breakdown possibilities, and inability to manage any self-care. This is all pretty impersonal and does not feel a bit like normal living. The idea is for the residents to make themselves at home in the facility. Having personal belongings that have value because they are theirs and because they bring back fond memories helps the new residents feel that the place is theirs. Having items that contribute to comfort and convenience also help to make the facility home.

PREPARING THE PLACE

If it is feasible, help your relative get her or his new home ready. You can do this by assisting with the selection of what is practical for him or her to take along and also what is meaningful and will enhance her or his life in ways that have nothing to do with practicality.

Get your relative's room ready for her or him with pictures, familiar and loved mementos, and items of interest that remind her or him of happy and successful events and lets others who see the objects know that your relative is an interesting and accomplished person. Do not be shy about posting honors and awards, art and craft work, pictures of vital, attractive people in interesting places or pursuits, or anything that defines the resident's life and personality. This will cause others to show interest, make favorable comments, and evince respect. Your relative will enjoy positive attention and feel better about him- or herself and her or his location.

If at all possible, prepare your relative's living space to be a personal place for him or her and make it as comfortable as you can. The more it looks and feels like home, the less of a shock it will be. Adjustment will be eased. Try to pave the way. Get the room ready before your relative moves into it.

At the same time, realize that each resident has limited storage space. Personal possessions are important, but the number of items possible is restricted. If your relative can tolerate change, a good solution is to rotate decorative accents, memorabilia, and clothes. Each new infusion provokes added interest from staff and other residents. This compounds the attention your relative receives.

CLOTHES

You can augment your relative's good feelings by paying close attention to the wardrobe. Comfortable clothes are an important consideration. Good repair and good looks need not be sacrificed.

Stylish clothes grab attention. The praise will help your relative's self-esteem. Even if the resident is disoriented he or she will still get the idea that he or she is being admired. Monitor your relative's clothing, making sure he or she is dressed carefully in matching, coordinated outfits and that the clothes are in good condition. You are the primary person to do this. Staff members will not attend to stains, small rips, and missing buttons. You want your relative to look better than adequate.

You will prefer to have your relative dressed in street clothes. The resident will feel and act better if he or she gets ready for the day as he or she would if he or she were planning on making a good impression and being involved with attractive people. At the same time, select attire that allows ease in dressing and is not difficult for the resident to handle. Be aware of your relative's special needs. Some residents can manage clothes with zippers in the front, but are unable to deal with buttons. Avoid difficult back fastenings. Dresses and shirts that pull on over the head are useful. Check with the staff, particularly the occupational and physical therapists, for clothing especially designed for people with disabilities and infirmities. There are garments with velcro closings and other adaptations that make it possible for residents to engage in self-care and be less dependent.

Clothing needs to be designed to meet the residents' needs. Some women are better off wearing slacks for warmth and for modesty as they do not keep skirts decorously arranged. Other women will appreciate slacks because they are more adaptable to their activities throughout the day.

Look around and note what the other residents are wearing. What looks most carefree, comfortable, yet eye-catching? The most popular outfits, for men and women, seem to be the terry cloth or velour jogging suits. They are attractive and residents get statements of admiration and envy from staff and visitors. They slip on or zip up and are easy to get on and off. They are soft, nonabrasive, and comfortable to wear. The material is cuddly looking so those outfitted in them get petted and hugged. They are easy to care for and do not wrinkle or need special handling. They stand up well. Even so, not everyone will like them. Preferences count. Some residents are at ease in their own familiar style of clothing even if it appears to be neither comfortable nor carefree. Self-image is of consequence, and the residents' idea of what their appearance should be is closely related to self-esteem.

An ongoing problem with the residents' wardrobe is the nursing home's laundry service. Their commercial-type laundry is very hard on clothes. If they can shrink, fade, stretch, or be damaged in any way, the laundry process will manage to do it. Equally as problematic is the clothing that never returns from the laundry. This can be prevented to some extent by marking each item of your relative's clothing with a pen that has ink that will not wash out, even with repeated washings. First initial and last name should be on everything that will go to the laundry, with clothing marked in an easily seen place, usually the neckline, but not so that it mars the apparel with unsightly identification. Socks can be marked on the toes, underwear on waist bands and fastenings. This should ensure return, but through some mystic event that seemingly baffles all involved, clothing still disappears. Sometimes it turns up weeks or months later. It has been found in the closets of other residents, or other residents have been seen wearing the garments. If it is possible, take your relative's laundry home, wash it, and return it to him or her. Even so, it should be marked with your relative's name. Circumstances may prevent you from caring for your relative's clothes. The handiest alternative is the facility's laundry service. Their fee is generally minimal. However, using it is fraught with frustration. You may want to address the problem with the administrator or through the Resident or Family Council. Perhaps you can come up with a solution. If so, you will reap nationwide gratitude. The present system, in most nursing homes, is unsatisfactory, and no one seems to be able to make it work right. It is a problem that should be corrected.

HELPFUL ITEMS

Since most people have not had experience with disability and nursing home living, it is not surprising that they do not know what items are permitted, recommended, and helpful. Some of them are

1. Carryalls that attach to a wheelchair or a walker. Wheeling a chair or ambulating with a walker monopolizes the arms and hands, leaving nothing free for carrying what is wanted. Carryalls are bags that can be tied or snapped to the front of the walker or the side of a wheelchair. They serve, as the name suggests, as a carryall for the articles that residents want with them. You may be able to get just what you want from the nursing home activity or social work department. Volunteers often make numbers of these handy devices and contribute them to the facility for the residents' use. They are easy to sew or can be fashioned from a plastic bag.

2. A quartz clock with large numbers and a lighted dial. A clock helps disoriented residents as it is a reality check. If the numbers are large, the residents with poor eyesight can see it

and the lighted dial makes it visible at night. A clock that needs winding is difficult for arthritic fingers to handle. A person with orientation problems will not remember to wind, or will overwind. Remember to replace the battery when it stops keeping time.

3. A quartz, large-numbered watch with expansion band. The same applies here. Not having to wind a watch is a relief and big numbers are easier to see. It is another aid to time orientation. The expansion band facilitates getting the watch off and on.

4. A change purse. Many of the residents like to carry a little money with them for the vending machine, stamps, or to purchase something from the small general store set up for residents in many facilities. A small change purse is exactly what is needed for such occasions.

5. A telephone. The facility has pay telephones that the residents can use. Some have portable telephones for the residents' convenience. Sometimes staff members will let the residents use the nursing home telephone and assist them with the call. If you want to call your relative frequently and the resident has friends and relatives in the community, a bedside telephone is essential to her or his social functioning. This is arranged privately and directly with the telephone company. The resident is responsible for the installation and the monthly bills. If you are worried about excessive calls do not go along with these arrangements. Also, keep in mind that every time your relative is moved to another room there will be charges for telephone installation all over again. If your relative gets a telephone, select one with programmable speed dialing and large push-button numbers.

6. Writing material. Keep your relative supplied with postcards and stamps, and if they have the energy and interest, writing paper and envelopes for longer letters. Postcards are quicker and an easier way to stay in touch. Greeting cards are nice as long as you help your relative remember special occasions. Making a thoughtful gesture, such as sending a birthday or get-well card, helps the resident focus on someone else and

104 | The Nursing Home Experience

connect with the lives of others. It is good reality orientation as he or she recalls people and dates that have impacted on his or her life.

7. A television set with ear phones. The day rooms have television sets, but it is not always easy to hear because of other activities. There may be conflict over which channel to watch. If the roommate has a television set, they may not want to watch the same programs at the same time. Ear phones will make it possible for your relative to watch whatever she or he wants when she or he wants it, and adjust the volume to her or his hearing comfort. Include a remote control for the set.

8. A VCR. The nursing home has a VCR and you can use theirs to show videos of family gatherings, weddings, baptisms, graduations, and other events that your relative could not attend, but will be pleased to have shared with her or him. If you have transferred old slides or home movies to video, the memories will be poignant and wonderful for your relative. If your relative likes to watch movies and you rent them for her or him regularly, his or her own VCR in the room will be just what she or he needs.

9. A radio. Does your relative like the music played by one or another radio station? Has the resident enjoyed the news or talk shows? Provide a radio with push-button station selection set on the numbers your relative wants so she or he can always push the same button with predictable results.

10. A cassette player and recorder, blank tapes, tapes of favorite music, and talking-book tapes. A cassette player is a useful tool as certain music, meditation, or relaxation tapes bring solace and comfort. Many residents like to listen to taped sermons and religious music. Talking-book tapes can be rented from the library and are an entertaining way for residents to pass the time, particularly if vision problems prevent reading. Blank tapes make it possible for the residents to record programs they want to listen to again or to use for communication with others. Residents' out-of-town relatives and friends may reply in kind with a talking letter. A tape of a cheerful, soothing female voice has been found to calm agitated residents with Alzheimer's disease.

11. Newspaper and/or magazine subscriptions. Getting mail on a regular basis is nice. Keeping up with what is happening will make your relative a more interesting person to you, others, and to him- or herself. If the resident cannot read all the paper, you can read some of it to her or him. This sharing and discussion of news might be a part of your regular visit to the nursing home. The best magazine subscriptions are pictorial or those in large print editions.

If it makes sense for your relative to get a newspaper, make sure that it gets delivered on a timely basis. The newspaper delivery is usually made to the front office of the nursing home. It can be delayed, misplaced, or misappropriated there. Monitor to establish a speedy dispatch of the newspaper to your relative after it arrives at the facility. Your relative should not have to wait or search for his or her own newspaper.

12. A plant. Something live and growing is nice to watch. It adds a homey feeling to the room. If the residents are able to care for them it gives them a responsibility. To that extent a plant can be therapeutic. If your relative cannot care for it by her- or himself, but she or he likes plants, you can tend it to bring him or her the pleasure. Check this out with the nursing home staff, as they may also be watering it. Decide who waters when. A healthy attractive plant tempts people into taking cuttings. Most residents thrive on giving these to staff members and visitors and like the attention it brings them. The plant will not be destroyed by this because an excessive number of cuttings will reduce its lusciousness and the requests for cuttings. It will have time to grow back. If it dies, it can be replaced.

13. A small stuffed animal or doll. Stuffed toys are cute, cuddly, and bring friendly comment from others. Residents often get a kick out of them. They are decorative. Some may appreciate their cuddly qualities. Large and numerous objects of any kind cannot be accommodated in the residents' rooms. They need space for moving around and for storage. The cleaning staff have problems with cumbersome items and clutter. So think small.

14. A sweater. Air-conditioned nursing homes are frequently a few degrees too cold for the people who live there. Even the

hard-working nursing staff are seen in sweaters. An attractive sweater or two that are comfortable and easy to wash will be welcomed and worn.

15. Regular hair-care appointments. Nothing seems to bring the residents more admiration than an attractive, well-groomed hair style. Set up and pay for regular, ongoing hair-care appointments. Unless the residents are confused and suspicious, they will look forward to this day and the results.

16. Warm socks and slippers. Feet get cold because of poor circulation and, in the case of wheelchair-bound residents, inactivity. Socks and slippers are a source of comfort. Some residents want to wear regular shoes when going out among others. That is a good policy. But cold, sore feet is such a negative that foot comfort needs to be given some priority. Help your relatives work out a way to combine comfort and style. Slacks, socks, and walking shoes are a generally acceptable combination.

17. A typewriter or computer. Typewriters and computers are electronic and compact. They are quiet and take little physical strength to use. Depending on what your relative did in the past, she or he may appreciate such a convenience for letter writing, keeping records, and in some instances, aiding in communication.

The Extras

18. Games, cards. Anything your relative can do alone will help pass the time. Word puzzles and hand-held, one-person coordination games are easy to store and use if your relative has the mental and manual dexterity. Cards and board games are popular. If you and your relative are able, you can entertain each other playing games during your visits. A running competition adds spice to life and is something to anticipate.

19. Food items. Food is generally not allowed in residents' rooms because it attracts bugs. Maybe prepackaged candies that your relative can share with staff and other residents will be permitted. The food ploy is an effective way to make friends and influence people.

Special treats of favorite foods are always welcomed. Do you make a desired food item? Shared edibles can make a routine visit an event worthy of remark.

20. Special occasions. Nursing home staff members will not remember the actual dates of birthdays, anniversaries, and other special occasions unless they are brought to their attention. The day can be made noteworthy by bringing eats for all, marking the milestone with balloons, showy greeting cards, or a party. Your relative will bask in the generated attention.

21. Pictures. Photos that bring fond memories and relate parts of your relative's life should already be in place. A new arrangement, attractive frames, or refurbishing and rotating pictures will reawaken interest in your relative, his or her friends, and the caretakers.

22. Cards. Even though you see your relative regularly, cards that can be read and reread are a delight. Pretty pictures and charming verses can be shown to others. Your added personal messages can be cherished. Inveigle relatives and friends who do not visit often to send messages by mail. If your relatives need mail read to them and you are not there to do it, seek out a person in the nursing home who will do this regularly. It could be someone from social services, activities, nursing, or a volunteer.

23. Hobby supplies. Hobbies may range from reading (large-print books are available) to crocheting to collecting to crafts. If there is some way and some form in which your relative can continue his or her hobbies and interests, get her or him the necessary supplies so the resident can have the satisfaction of prolonging the pursuit.

24. Decorate the room. Decorate your relative's room for the season or the holiday unless the resident is disoriented and this would cause added confusion and too much stimulation. In that case, maybe one small reminder of a recognized holiday will be enough to aid in reality orientation. Your alert, oriented relative will thrill to the festive appointments.

25. Humorous items. Funny plaques, statues, and cards are frivolous, but add spice to life. Stimulate your relative with

something that will cause a chuckle. She or he will have fun sharing the laugh with others. The merriment will be reexperienced each time someone else is involved in seeing it.

26. Self-help aids. Think velcro, adaptive eating, grooming, and dressing tools. What will help a person with one good hand, poor vision, difficult ambulation, hearing problems, speech impairments, and loss of memory function more easily and independently? Talk with the therapists in the facility, visit medical equipment stores, read library books on rehabilitation, and ask at the rehabilitation center. They have brochures and literature not available to the general public. Do not purchase any expensive equipment without an evaluation and checking with your relative's caregivers. They can be more objective than you about the usefulness of self-help devices you suggest.

27. A lapboard. A soft-sided lapboard is a great space saver for residents without a handy desk, but are additionally good for people who cannot hold books or need a lap-held writing or working space. You will like it so well you will buy one for yourself.

28. A bulletin board. A bulletin board makes it easier to put up holiday decorations, the activity schedule, photos, upcoming appointments, cards, favors and remembrances of parties attended, and newspaper articles.

29. A guest book. Ask all visitors to sign their names, make a short comment, and date their visits. This book becomes a source of pride, interest, and reference for the nursing home resident.

30. A full-length mirror. Residents do not get an opportunity to view themselves in a full-length mirror. It is good for morale and for taking responsibility if they are able to survey the self in total and check for posture, arrangement of clothes, and overall effect.

PROBLEMS WITH POSSESSIONS

The laundry lament has already been addressed. The problem of clothes lost and ruined in the laundry can be remedied only by adequate marking or laundry services outside the facility. If your relative is in a nursing home where laundry losses are not a problem, do not move her or him, praise the skilled people who run the laundry, and encourage them to teach others how to do as well as they do.

Personal possessions, as you know, are limited by space. There may also be regulations about hanging pictures on the walls and door decorations. Ask about these before your pound your first nail.

Do not have anything of value at the facility that cannot be replaced or locked up safely. Jewelry, glasses, hearing aids, and dentures are constantly lost, misplaced, or stolen.

Rings may be loose and fall off fingers and get thrown into the laundry with the bed clothes or sucked up in the vacuum cleaner. They may be seen as valuable by staff members who are untrustworthy, and stolen. Other residents may wander into the room and take things on purpose, by mistake, or in confusion. Consequently, heirloom or expensive jewelry should be insured if brought to the facility, locked up in a personal safe or the nursing home safe, or left at home or in a safety deposit box. Report all losses and thefts to nursing home personnel. They will be as eager as you to apprehend any thief and retrieve the valued possessions.

Eye glasses, dentures, and hearing aids are a special frustration that seems to be as universal as the laundry problem. They go out on lunch trays, are left in the common rooms, thrown into the garbage, flushed down the toilet, and picked up by other residents. And as much as these aids disappear, they accumulate at the nursing station. Sacks of unidentified dentures and glasses kept there sometimes produce the missing item, but more often are unwanted by anyone.

All aids should be engraved. This includes dentures, glasses, and hearing aids. This provides a means of identification. The residents should be trained always to put their appliances in the same place. No one should be allowed to rearrange these articles. If they can be covered by an insurance policy, insure them. Get cords so glasses can stay around the neck. Learn your relative's habits so you can set up measures to prevent loss at what appears to be likely times for this to happen. One woman took her husband's hearing aids with her when she left the facility and returned them when she arrived for her next visit.

110 | The Nursing Home Experience

This prevented loss, but also kept him from hearing anyone he lived with. There must be better solutions.

When such problems, or others, occur, organize to get a procedure in place so the residents get what they need. If more than a procedure is required, if it is people, services, or things, work to help the nursing home get them. Use your knowledge and your caring to make the nursing home experience better for everyone, and, should you ever need it yourself, you will have made it something that you can anticipate without dread.

LIST OF ITEMS YOUR RELATIVE MAY NEED AND ENJOY

1. Pictures
2. Mementos
3. Trophies and citations
4. Art and craft work
5. Comfortable, stylish, easy-to-handle clothing
6. Laundry marking pen
7. Carryalls for walkers and wheelchairs
8. Quartz clock with large, lighted dial
9. Quartz, large-numbered watch
10. Small change purse
11. Large-numbered, push-button telephone with speed dialing
12. Writing material
13. Television with earphones
14. VCR
15. Radio with push-button dialing
16. Cassette player and recorder and tapes
17. Newspaper and magazine subscriptions
18. Plant
19. Stuffed animal or doll
20. Warm sweater
21. Regular hair-care appointments
22. Warm socks and slippers
23. Typewriter or computer
24. Games and cards
25. Food items
26. Special-occasion celebrations
27. Photos that bring back happy memories
28. Hobby supplies
29. Large-print books
30. Seasonal decorations for the room

31. Humorous cards or items
32. Self-help aids
33. Lapboard
34. Bulletin board
35. Guest book
36. Small room safe
37. Full-length mirror

5

Visiting Techniques

Visiting nursing home residents is allowed at any time and is encouraged. Visits may be at your convenience, but the residents may have other engagements. Medical attention may be scheduled in the form of physicians' appointments and therapies or procedures. They may have hair-care appointments or need personal help from a nursing assistant. The agenda for these attentions can only be minimally adjusted, so plan your time around them.

Time your visit to correspond with the resident's activity program so he or she can feel free to attend whatever he or she wants. Take nap, rest, getting-up and going-to-bed times into consideration. You may not want to visit at meal times.

You end up trying to fit your schedule with the resident's. Both of you have preferences. Negotiate to get what you both want. Visiting should be when you both have time to devote to each other and can maintain interest without getting bored or irritated.

Over 50 percent of all nursing home residents have daily or weekly visitors. A quarter of the residents have less frequent visitors. A little over 10 percent have no visitors at all.

How often you visit depends on your time, where you live, the resident's diagnosis, and other priorities. Think about your own schedule, how often you saw your relative before nursing home placement, and how often you think you should visit now. Know what you can do and do that. Maybe you cannot care for the relative in your home, but you can visit. Maybe you cannot visit regularly, but you can call, write, or contact the nursing home. If you live in another area, far flung from where your relative lives, you may want to hire a case manager. A case manager visits regularly to make sure your relative is well cared for and has what he or she needs. The case manager becomes an advocate, a friend, and a confidant and reports directly to you. There may be case managers listed in the yellow pages of your telephone book under social service organizations or social workers. They usually work with a network, so there are people to assist residents domiciled in various parts of the nation. The service will be called something similar to case management, life care, or caring continuum services. If you cannot find one, ask the social worker in your relative's nursing home if a case manager sees people in the facility. If not, the facility's social work consultant might fill this role, or any social worker in private practice in the area can do it. Ask the nursing home social worker to send you a telephone-book listing of the local social workers so you can contact them and determine their services and their fees. You may want to request that the nursing home social worker introduce the idea to several of the area social workers to see if one of them would consent to being a case manager.

The frequency of visits is significant, but the quality of visits is more important. One pleasant, memorable visit outweighs scads of unpleasant, humdrum visits. The mutual support that is achieved through effective visiting has been proven to be a factor in the residents' health. Having someone who cares and to whom they can talk strengthens the residents' natural immune system. Residents and families need to dwell more on the positive aspects of having a continued relationship and less on the unwanted changes. Children have their grandparents, adult children their parents, husbands, and wives, their spouses, and friends, their ongoing affinity. Even if people change substantially—and people do change—the relationship can continue.

Family visits are more than a time to check on your relative and a chance for a quick hello. They are an opportunity to bring in the outside world and to assist the resident in dealing with staff and nursing home policies and procedures. Relatives and friends are fond symbols of the link between the past and the present.

VISITING TIPS

Your visits with your relative will have to be arranged to meet your mutual physical and emotional needs. Setting the time and frequency comes first. Then you can think about what to do during the visits. Some of the following suggestions are general and will suit any relative. Others are for residents with particular problems.

1. Provide a calendar for visits. Write in visits as they happen and as they are planned. This helps your relative remember that you visited and will again. This is also a good reference for staff members who can look to see when you will be available if they need to talk with you. It helps with reality orientation for the confused resident and is a tangible reminder that you are involved in his or her life.

2. Report on yourself. Do you have new clothes, a new hairdo? Have you been somewhere? Are there accomplishments or disappointments? Residents tend to become insular, thinking only of their own lives and schedules. Be the link to the community for your relative. Remind him or her that you have a multidimensional life with other interests, people, problems, pleasures, and responsibilities. You life consists of more than visiting the nursing home. Your relative's life should be much more than just your visits.

3. Involve your relative in the family. Do not protect your relative from upsetting news. This shuts her or him out from authentic emotional involvement and makes the relationship artificial and strained. People who are involved with each other and love each other have shared good and bad news for years and should continue the same pattern of participation. Certainly you want your relative to be happy, but preventing him or her from being an integral part of what is going on is not the way to do it. He or she will feel left out and closed out. If your relative picks up any indication that all is not well, what he or she imagines will always be worse than the facts. The relative loses the comfort of mutual support if he or she cannot discuss with you what is going on. He or she worries fruitlessly and alone.

4. Involve your relative in decision making. If the relative has always been part of the family decision-making process it is

essential that this role continue. If this is taken away it constitutes another loss. The resident who loses a status role within the family gets angry and depressed and feels as though he or she is not needed. If the relative can no longer make the ultimate decision, at least he or she can voice an opinion or contribute to some part of the process. If he or she can manage nothing more, he or she should at least be told of the decision.

5. Mark belongings. Use the visit time for various helpful projects, such as making sure the resident's personal items are ALL marked with appropriate (will not wash or fall off) identification. The identification needs to be on everything, including wheelchairs and other self-help appliances, furniture, decorative items, and even possessions that are used daily and are eventually used up.

6. Stimulate the senses. There are five senses: sight, sound, taste, smell, and touch. As people age, any or all of the senses become less acute. You can help your relative develop, compensate for, and enjoy the senses. If you notice sensory changes you can report this to the nursing department. You are more likely than they to notice problems since you are more tuned in to your relative and are not with him or her every day, all day long.

   a. Sight. If your relative cannot see well, what does he or she need to compensate for the loss? Will large print, bold colors, emphasis on what he or she can feel and hear, do it?

   b. Sound. Make sure your relative can understand what you have to say by sitting where he or she can see your lips move. Talk in a low, slow voice. Clean the hearing aids and make sure the batteries are working. Adapt equipment as much as possible. Get the telephone modified for the hearing-impaired and provide head phones for the television and radio. If your relative is in a coma, tell stories or read to him or her. Use a pleasant, soothing voice. Hearing is the last sense to go.

   c. Taste. The taste buds are not the same in the elderly as they are in a younger person. Spruce up bland foods with interesting, not necessarily spicy, seasonings. Older people are often drawn to sweets as the sweet taste is more pronounced and, thus, more satisfying. If sugar is not contraindicated, bring in treats to celebrate your visit. If sugar is a problem, find a sugar-free confection as a gift.

d. Smell. Certain smells evoke special memories. Gardenias may bring back the high school prom, moth balls, the advent of fall, or pipe tobacco the recollection of a favorite uncle. Have a feast of smells, perfumes, foods, flowers, cleaning agents—and discuss the thoughts they conjure up. This is particularly effective for residents suffering from organic brain syndromes or for those who are comatose. Pick smells that you think will dredge up happy thoughts and comforting feelings.

e. Touch. People orient to touch more than to the other senses. Hugs and pats of affection are immediately translated into approval, caring, and good feelings. As much as residents are around people all the time, individualized personal contact does not take place. Even when the residents receive personal care because they cannot manage their own self-care, the physical contact is not like that received from a favored friend or relative who bestows hugs and pats out of love and concern, and not because it is part of a job. Think about using lotion to give a relaxing back rub. Comatose residents may respond to the feel of velvet or some other sort or stimulating object.

7. Stimulate both sides of the brain. The left side of the brain works with facts and figures; the right side of the brain works with intuition and feelings. The dominant left side produces the bookkeepers and the technicians. The right side is the seat of art, invention, and fantasy. Your relative may become less able to generalize, abstract, fantasize as he or she ages. You can help her or him stay alert and have more fun by indulging in flights of fancy with him or her, having the relative draw, work with clay, think of ten uses for a toothpick, or make up stories. Brainstorm with her or him, allowing suggestions to be as silly and incredible as they can be.

Stimulate the left side of the brain by balancing your or your relative's checkbook. Talk about the uses of new words. Fit them into a sentence. Play trivia. Tell the resident of something you are going to do together and have the expectation that he or she will remember. Assist the memory by writing it down, having him or her write it down, reminding her or him, and asking questions to trigger the memory.

8. Laugh together. Laughter is relaxing, creates a bond, gives an exclamation mark to the day, and is good exercise. It is internal jogging. Recall funny events that you and your relative have shared. Report amusing anecdotes. Bring in cartoons and comics that elicit merriment. Learn and tell jokes. Collect them from friends, books, and magazines. Do the same if you write letters: enclose a humorous saying, a joke, or a cartoon.

9. Recap your vacation. Share the videos and pictures of your vacation trip. Tell about it. Let your relative know what you learned, what you liked. Make a cassette tape each day you are away and send the tapes to your relative as you travel along. Do not forget the picture postcards.

10. Make telephone calls. Your visit might be a good time to place telephone calls to favorite friends and relatives, both local and away. This is something you and your relative can share and enjoy.

11. Bring news of the family. Try to keep your relative's world from becoming increasingly smaller. Tell her or him the progress of children and grandchildren. Or concentrate one visit on one child, using photographs that show changes as the little one grows and a tape or video showing the child's verbal ability.

12. Listen to music. Most people have favorite music. Listen to it with your relative. Music is calming to agitated residents. It will be relaxing and pleasurable for both of you. Music that is cheerful is helpful for the depressed person. Music is therapy as well as enjoyment.

13. Read poems. Does your relative like poems or inspirational essays? Read them to the resident. Discuss them. Leave the ones that are especially liked with your relative. Your relative may want to bring them to someone else's attention.

14. Help the disoriented. If your relative is disoriented and easily confused and distracted, make sure you identify yourself and what you are doing. Try to fit into the resident's routine by visiting at the same time and the same day and indulging in

familiar and nonthreatening routine, such as having a food treat together, going for a walk or wheelchair ride around or outside the facility. Do the same things each visit. Be predictable. When your relative is confused remind him or her of the reality by gently stating the facts. If your relative becomes upset or overreacts, do not argue or get insistent. Stay calm and reassuring.

15. Learn from your relative. Your elderly relative knows more about being old than you do. You can learn from your relative. Nursing home residents are also good sources of historical information about the community, the country, and the family. Have a set of questions prepared so that you or your relative can record the information on tape, in writing, or just to use as a springboard to an interesting conversation. If the information is recorded, make copies because it will be valuable to friends, relatives, and the historical society.

16. Explore. Investigate the nursing home. You and your relative can locate all the specialized places in the facility, note changes in decorations and decor, and see where the staff members have their offices. Explore the nursing home neighborhood if your relative can make forays with you. Are there parks, shops, restaurants, churches, near by? What is there to see and do? Give your relative a complete picture of the nursing home and the surroundings.

17. Visit your home. If your relative can visit outside the facility, arrange a visit to your home on special occasions and as appropriate. It feels good to be in a comfortable and familiar place, and this is a break from the usual routine. Your relative will appreciate the continuity of the home and family as he or she visits your home and family now and then.

18. Go on outings. Use visits as an occasion for outings. Once a week or once a month eat in a restaurant, visit a shopping center, sit in the park. Stimulate the senses, make the world a little larger, break into the monotony, give your relative something to think and talk about.

19. Tell the truth. A relative in a nursing home may ask difficult and repetitious questions dealing with wanting to leave the facility or wondering where he or she is. Be kind. Be gentle. Be honest. Be prepared. Always explain that the resident needs

more care than you can give. State that the nursing home is now his or her home and you will always visit and help look out for the resident's well-being.

20. Listen to feelings. Your relative's feelings are important. If the resident can express feelings to you it helps because an empathetic ear is the best device there is for making a person feel loved and understood. You may not be able to change anything, but you can exhibit caring. That may be enough.

Residents sometimes express their feelings indirectly. Complaints about the nursing home may really be expressions of unhappiness with their life, health, relationships. When addressing the complaints does not solve the problems, give attention, recognition, caring, instead.

21. Make it special. Bring a special tea set, flowers, or a lovely serving set to use for sharing an elegant lunch. It will be worth the effort if it brightens your relative's day and gives you the satisfaction of a meaningful visit.

22. Bring children. Children are natural and friendly around older people and are infrequently seen in a nursing home. Children expect to like and be liked and it works out that way. You may need to prepare children by explaining what a nursing home is and give them opportunities while there to ask questions. Also allow them to discuss the visit afterward. Do not make the visit long as the young and old tire easily. If the child is prepared to dance, sing, or recite, encourage the little artist to perform.

23. Arrange pet visits. Pets make great visitors. They are happy to cuddle and be petted. Residents who will respond to little else will reach out to hold a puppy or a kitten.

24. Play games. If you and your relative played games or cards before the placement, continue this practice after the placement. It keeps the visits natural and continues the relationship as it was. If you never played games before, and the relationship seems difficult, you might try a game to see if it helps to have something to do during the visit. Card games, dominoes, or a board game can be the basis for an ongoing competition.

25. Keep your promises. Visit when you said you would. Take your relative out as planned. Do what you promised to do. Be reliable and trustworthy.

26. Go to church. Many residents enjoy going to a "real" church. They prefer this to attending the services in the facility. It somehow seems better to worship in a familiar sanctuary. If this is possible for your relative, arrange your visits to include occasional or regular church attendance.

27. Plan with the staff. When you plan a special visit or outing let the nursing home staff know so they can have space prepared or your relative ready to go, with proper doses of medication. They and your relative need to know the expected time of return.

28. Plan your visit. Review what works and what does not. What did you do during pleasant visits? What has been upsetting for your relative? How did you handle it? What might you do better? Make notes of what you want to accomplish. Write down what you want to remember to tell your relative. List anecdotes you want to relate.

29. Do a make-over. If your relative is a female, go armed with perfume, powder, lipstick, and other makeup items. Both of you can experiment with new colors and styles.

30. Read aloud. Read short stories. Start a novel and read from it at each visit. Read the newspaper or a special interest magazine. Both of you can learn and be entertained at the same time.

31. Write letters. Send cards. If your relative cannot write, write letters as he or she dictates them. Remember special friends and relatives and send out greeting cards with your relative, not for your relative.

32. Dine together. Purchase a meal at the nursing home and eat with your relative in the room, in the dining room, or on the patio. Your relative will see you as a guest and you will get to sample the nursing home food.

33. Take a tour of the town. Look at the old neighborhood. Show the new buildings, developments, and additions to the

town. Communities always have some changes and your relative may be fascinated with them. It is part of keeping up to date with what is going on and contributes to your relative's being a more alert and interesting person.

34. Praise. Keep your complaints about the facility to yourself until you can talk to the appropriate staff person. Praise what you can about the nursing home so your relative can take pride in the surroundings.

35. Reminisce. If your relative has short-term memory loss, reminiscing may be the best approach you have. The resident will remember the past and take pleasure in recounting former exploits and incidents. You will leave with good feelings and an enriched knowledge of the family history.

36. Take a day at a time. Your relative's moods and physical status may change from day to day. If one visit was not good, figure out how to make the next one better. If you notice a slow deterioration, you must realize that, once you confirm that it is not a curable disease, it may well be something you cannot prevent and will have to accept.

37. Practice problem solving. Do not solve problems for your relative, but be available to help by assisting in the listing of alternatives and exploring possible results of various approaches. Residents need this kind of help and learn to expand their options and take more control of their lives when this is done.

38. Use communication aids. A relative who has a severe communication problem because of diminished vision or hearing or as a consequence of a progressive disease or a stroke is a special challenge. Set up a communication system for the two of you. You may be able to use flash cards, computers, communications boards, eye, hand, or head signals, or sign language. Once an effective means of exchanging messages is developed, make sure nursing home personnel know about it.

39. Go to an activity. Plan your visit around a nursing home activity that you and your relative can attend together. You help your relative integrate into the facility and a difficult visit can be eased if there is something to do. Bingo is always popular, but

122 | The Nursing Home Experience

there are exercises, crafts, singalongs, and many spectator and social events.

40. Touch. Give your relative a hug. A special hug from a special person may be the highlight of the visit.

41. Practice your skill. If you know or are learning to play a musical instrument, perfect some type of handwork, or anything at all, give a demonstration to your relative. You will have some practice time. Your relative will have an intriguing visit.

42. Ask questions. What is your favorite sport? What is the best game you ever saw? What is your favorite color? Do you remember the nicest present you ever received? Tell about your favorite job, vacation, hobby. Where did you most like to live? You will find out things you never knew about your relative and have a fascinating visit.

43. Start a scrapbook. Mementos of days gone by are necessary and nice. But your relative should live in the present. Start a scrapbook related to what is happening now. There will be many family and nursing home events, pictures, favors, and newsletter mentions that can be put in the book to remind your relative that life continues to be interesting.

44. Encourage your relative to keep a journal or a cassette of everyday experiences. If your relative makes a point of reporting events so that they are available to you when you visit, he or she will be more tuned in to the particulars and patterns of the days.

45. Work on a puzzle. You may enjoy doing a crossword or any other word puzzle together. A jigsaw puzzle is a comfortable project for a twosome. The resident can put in some pieces between visits or you can work companionably together. You may have a problem finding a place to keep it set up and out of the way over a period of time.

46. Let your relative teach you. Does your relative make fish lures, talk French, or tie knots? Get him or her to teach you. He or she will feel useful. You will grow in knowledge.

47. Write. Even though you see your relative regularly, he or she will love to get mail and cards. Letters and cards can be read

over and over and shown to others. Sharing information through writing (visually) and again through visiting (auditorily) helps your relative understand and retain what you are explaining. You will feel that your message was heard with this two-channel approach.

48. Telephone. Short, frequent calls—between visits or if you cannot visit—can be part of any feeling-good program. This can only be done, of course, if your relative has a telephone, can talk on the phone, or has easy access to the public telephone. Long telephone calls are tiring and repetitive. Have a short, cheery agenda and say good-bye.

49. Give gifts. Gifts at the appropriate time are great, but little remembrances throughout the year make any occasion a special one. Try to make them small, usable, disposable, or consumable so your relative's available space does not get cluttered.

50. Remember special joys. Try to remember your relative's special joys and cater to them on occasion. What makes him or her happy? Is it more information on a favorite movie star? Is it anything in a preferred color? If you do not know, find out.

51. Tape the visit. Sometimes the resident forgets the family visited and complains that they never come by. Keeping a calendar and marking visits will help the staff members remind the resident of the regular contacts. Making a cassette tape or video will recall the visit to your relative. It can be a short statement of date and time, a few of the topics discussed, and a reminder of the next visit. If she or he can see her- or himself actually visiting with you on a video it can effectively soothe him or her. And he or she can relive the experience.

52. Tape everybody. Make videos of family events your relative cannot attend. Tape visits you make to faraway grandchildren. Have relatives and friends send videos showing off their talents and/or telling the resident what the resident means to them. Maybe they can recall a memorable experience.

53. Enjoy television together. If you watch a certain soap opera and your relative in the nursing home does also, watch it together. If you cannot arrange that, it can be the basis for an ongoing conversation as you discuss the ins and outs of the plot

and the characters. Maybe the program you select to watch and discuss will be a sitcom, a spy, or a sports program. Work on this commonality.

54. Bring in the world. Your relative may not be able to reach outside the nursing home, but you can bring the world to the resident by relating what is happening with family, neighborhood, community, country, the world. Bring more than facts. Report opinions and analysis. Make sure you get your relative's reaction. Residents who are more involved in the world around them and know what is going on are more respected by others and feel more in control of their lives. Knowing is right up there with doing.

55. Celebrate a special event. Remember the milestones so that your relative can be the guest of honor at an event in her or his honor. People blossom when they are the center of attention for an important reason.

56. Label drawers and closets. When adjusting to a new environment it is hard to remember where everything is. Label the drawers and closets. If your relative is disoriented include pictures as well as words to indicate what is where.

57. Compliment. Be sure to give one compliment or one statement of appreciation at each visit. Even if you have to dig deep it will be well worth the morale building you are doing. Residents do better in an atmosphere of caring and approval.

58. Be attentive. Being there is not enough. Your relative needs to know he or she has your undivided attention. Make eye contact. Ask follow up questions. Smile and nod at the right times.

59. Be positive. Do not get bogged down in guilt, resentment, and self-blaming. Do not focus on the negative aspects of group living. Make your visit a positive occasion.

60. Make a toast. If medically allowed, enjoy a cocktail with your relative. For many this adds a touch of conviviality.

61. Bring out the child. Stop at the toy department and stock up. Depending on your relative's level of functioning the toys

you select will feel appropriate or playing with them will feel like a time to let go and just have fun. Bubble-making solution and wands are a treat and can be used on the patio and indoors. Do not bypass silly putty and the paddles with the balls attached to them. You will both relax and giggle and feel joy. These toys also help with coordination, and using them exercises muscles.

62. Pray or meditate. A common religious belief can be a comfort and a strength to both of you. Prayer is restful. If you are not religious, meditation is helpful for clearing the mind, releasing worries, and regaining perspective.

Do not quit with these suggestions. Find techniques that work for you and your relative so each of you regards visiting as a good experience, one that both of you look forward to, and that neither feels is a burden. Keep the following four tips in mind when planning your visits.

1. Schedule time that is right for you and the resident.
2. Stay only as long as you need to accomplish the purpose of your visit.
3. Make the visit mutually entertaining and positive.
4. Evaluate after each visit to determine what went right and to plan the next visit.

List of Visiting Tips

1. Provide a calendar for visits
2. Report on yourself
3. Involve your relative in the family
4. Involve your relative in decision making
5. Mark belongings
6. Stimulate the senses
7. Stimulate both sides of the brain
8. Laugh together
9. Recap your vacation
10. Make telephone calls
11. Bring news of the family
12. Listen to music
13. Read poems
14. Help the disoriented

126 | The Nursing Home Experience

15. Learn from your relative
16. Explore
17. Visit your home
18. Go on outings
19. Tell the truth
20. Listen to feelings
21. Make it special
22. Bring children
23. Arrange pet visits
24. Play games
25. Keep your promises
26. Go to church
27. Plan with the staff
28. Plan your visit
29. Do a make-over
30. Read aloud
31. Write letters, send cards
32. Dine together
33. Take a tour of the town
34. Praise
35. Reminisce
36. Take a day at a time
37. Practice problem solving
38. Use communication aids
39. Go to an activity
40. Touch
41. Practice your skill
42. Ask questions
43. Start a scrapbook
44. Encourage your relative to keep a journal or a cassette of everyday experiences
45. Work on a puzzle
46. Let your relative teach you
47. Write
48. Telephone
49. Give gifts
50. Remember special joys
51. Tape the visit
52. Tape everybody
53. Enjoy television together
54. Bring in the world
55. Celebrate a special event
56. Label drawers and closets

57. Compliment
58. Be attentive
59. Be positive
60. Make a toast
61. Bring out the child
62. Pray or meditate

6

The Nursing Home Staff

Besides helping your relative select a nursing home, adjust to a new lifestyle, and stay in touch with the outside world, you can help the resident get better care by knowing how to work with the nursing home staff. They, after all, are crucial to whether or not the facility provides what your relative needs and wants.

THE STAFF'S RESPONSIBILITIES AND VIEWPOINTS

Every nursing home staff member is important to the care of your relative, but some are far more important than others. In terms of day-to-day care and contact, the nursing assistants are the most vital people in your relative's life.

A nursing assistant sees your relative every single day. The nursing assistant bathes, grooms, dresses, toilets, supervises for safety, helps with food trays and feeding, makes beds, and checks weight and vital signs. Your relative counts on the nursing assistants for the needs of everyday living. Because of what nursing assistants do, residents become dependent on them. The assistants' moods and attitudes influence those of the resident. The assistants become a source of emotional support.

The nursing assistants know more about your relative than anyone else in the facility. They hear the residents' plans, hopes, and fantasies. They know how to handle the residents to get them to do what has to be done. They know what upsets them, which are the problem areas, and what gives them pleasure. They know more about you, even though they may never have seen you, than you may want anyone to know. The nursing assistants bear the brunt of the residents' disappointments, dismay, and displeasure. They deal with the threatened, angry, and disoriented residents. They clean people up, settle people down, are responsible for how attractive your relative looks, and make the difference between satisfaction and discontent. You want to know these people and have them take an interest in your relative.

Most states now require that nursing assistants be certified. This means they must complete a course of specific training that prepares them for the work they do. You will hear them called CNAs—certified nursing assistants. Give them respect and consideration. They deserve it.

The nursing assistants become fond of the many residents with whom they interact. The residents who are cheerful and appreciative and have engaging personalities are especially appealing. The nursing assistant will be on the residents' side and believe any complaints they have about their relatives. You may be the most wonderful, attentive relative in the world, but if the CNAs hear that you are not what your relative would like you to be, they will sympathize with the resident and wish you would do what the resident thinks would make him or her happy. They will be glad to meet you and know that you are concerned. They want to hear what you have to say. You may have to meet and orient new assistants continually because the turnover is depressingly frequent.

The nursing assistants are supervised by a registered nurse. There is a nursing hierarchy in a nursing home, as there is in every medical facility. There are charge nurses at each nursing station, sometimes more than one, depending on the number of residents and staff. They change with every shift, three times in twenty-four hours. Each shift may see your relative from a different perspective. You may want to check with them all. These charge nurses give the assignments and orders to the certified nursing assistants and supervise their work. They are the people to talk to regarding the direct delivery of care to your relative.

Restorative nursing is a separate section of the nursing department. It is devoted to physical and rehabilitative therapy. The staff of this department makes it possible for residents to be more independent. They work to restore old skills and help the residents learn new adaptive ones.

The charge nurses report to the nursing supervisors who in turn are responsible to the assistant director of nursing and the director of nursing. All these positions are filled by college-trained registered nurses. They have their degree, have passed a state test for a license, and are required to obtain many hours of additional training every year to keep their licenses valid. Most of them have had a great deal of experience in geriatric nursing and in nursing homes. They are well versed in nursing home administration, supervision of medical staff, federal and state rules and regulations, and the medical and emotional needs and problems of the nursing home resident.

The nursing staff has more influence on your relative's daily schedule and well-being than do members of any other specialty employed in the nursing home. They decide what will be done and when. They set the tone. They can be demanding or lax. They can be accommodating or rigid. They can see you as part of the care team or intrusive. You want to set the stage so they want to help you and your relative.

The activity department staff are also involved with your relative on a daily basis, but less obviously. Activities permeate a facility, but families are not always aware of how much of the residents' lives may be involved with this department and its staff. When you are not at the nursing home your relative may be enjoying a variety of organized groups and entertainments or have personally prescribed, room-delivered therapeutic diversions. Talk to the activity director to determine what your relative does for recreation. You may learn something you can use for your visits or you may be able to contribute to the activity plan for the resident.

Activity employees are frequently important to residents because they are usually friendly, outgoing, persuasive people. In some instances the residents find the activity coordinator/director to be the person who means the most to them because the activity specialist is a source of pleasure and stimulation, working along with the residents to help them obtain self-esteem from their participation in the activity department.

You never know whom the residents will pick as the employee who means the most to them. It may be the nursing assistant, the nurse, the activity coordinator, the social worker, the special therapist, the administrator, the custodian, or any of the staff members or volunteers. Find this out from your relative, if he or she can tell you, or from the staff, and express appreciation to the person for the interest and kindness displayed. He or she will like your approbation and work harder to live up to your gratitude and respect.

The activity department offers at least one organized activity every day, and most often two or three. This is quite amazing considering the fact that, in most nursing homes, this department is staffed with only one or two people. They must rely on volunteers to provide programs and classes and to transport residents to and from the activity rooms.

Employees in the activity programs range from people with a special skill, such as in ceramics, to college-trained recreational therapists.

The social service department staff are devoted to problem solving and want to see you and your relative content and benefiting from the nursing home experience. They are often the residents' confidants and help them with their concerns. They are the people to see if you have a problem you do not know how to solve. They can direct and assist you. The social workers may be advocates on your behalf to the other staff, but do not count on it. All the department heads report to the administrator, who has the authority. Since the staff all have to work together, they are usually supportive of each other and will not accuse another staff member or go out on a limb on your behalf. They, after all, have to keep working together after your problem is settled.

The social worker will have a college degree in social work. Many will have master's degrees. This department sometimes includes responsibilities for admissions and marketing. When this is the case, the social worker is spread too thin to be the supportive person you generally could expect him or her to be.

The administrator is the boss and makes the final decisions. She or he will have experience and education in health-care administration and be licensed by the state. Administrators perform no hands-on care and have contact with the residents only

132 | The Nursing Home Experience

if they are so inclined by personality and work habits and if they have the time. The administrator may be seen out and about the facility or may never be seen, depending on the individual's personal style. You want this person to know what you value and appreciate. The administrator can emphasize certain programs and reward employees who do well. No question should be too small, nor should you feel at the mercy of busy staff. If you are puzzled and cannot find answers, expect the administrator to help you.

You will want to talk to other department heads on occasion. You will see the dietitian, who has a college degree in nutrition and is licensed, about your relative's diet. The housekeeping department will claim your attention when an emergency cleanup is required. The less you see a need for housekeeping the better they are doing their job. When they are taken for granted it is because they are keeping everything clean and orderly.

Get acquainted with the laundry process, usually part of the housekeeping department, if you plan to have the nursing home staff care for your relative's clothes, because you will be asking them to locate misplaced items.

Medical records will require your relative's signature, or yours if you are the responsible party, to release medical information from the facility to anyone else.

The maintenance department is another department that is not noticed when they are doing a bang-up job. If everything is working and in good repair, no one gives them a second thought. They are good people to know should you want some special adaptation or accommodation. Maintenance department employees have been known to be quite creative in building something specific to aid the residents.

Your relative's physician is not on the nursing home staff, but works through the nursing home staff in diagnosing and treating your relative. This is good and bad. It is good as the nurses enlarge on the doctor's information, but the doctor may be so rushed that he or she may not give the residents individual attention, relying on staff information instead. You may need to personalize your relative for the medical doctor.

This short summary should give you a clear impression that nursing home staff members are

1. In jobs specifically designed to help the residents and their families.
2. Educated for their positions.
3. Busy.

Just as each resident is different, so is each staff member. Personalities can mesh or clash. Even as personalities vary, so do abilities. Everyone does not do all things well. Neither does each staff member have equal skill in dealing with all kinds of emotional problems. Some of the staff may be able to tolerate repetitious questions with equanimity. Others may have just the right approach for the agitated resident. Unfortunately, they do not have the luxury of deciding with whom they will work. And as professionals they are usually quite hard on themselves, expecting that they should be able to handle all situations well. Thus, they may be easily threatened when mistakes or matters of poor judgment are brought to their attention. This is doubly difficult when they are doing their best, feel they are getting no appreciation, and fear they are being judged unjustly. These staff members are there when residents are upset after the family members leave, and when family members gather up a long list of complaints, springing them all at once, and when the residents complain to the family, but tell the staff that everything is fine.

Staff members enjoy working with the residents and sometimes see the family members as necessary evils. All seems to go well until the family complicates matters. The truth of the matter is that it is easier to work with an individual, the resident, than with a group, the family. When staff members feel threatened by family members they sometimes get defensive rather than cooperative. Wise family members make sure they build a trusting relationship with staff. This does not mean constant approval. It means being part of the team with the ability to problem-solve when the need arises.

WHEN TO COMMUNICATE WITH THE STAFF

Communication with the staff should be pleasant, open, and ongoing so it will not appear that you are only interested in complaining and criticizing. Not that this is easy. You will have to go out of your way to state a cheery hello or job well done as everyone always seems occupied and tied up with the job at hand. This does not mean that you need to be a nuisance, engaging the staff in lengthy, time-consuming conversations. But do notice them and make sure they notice you. Communicate plans and concerns. Ask questions and express worries. Do not imply that they have done wrong until you know that that is the case. That is your last alternative.

Talk with staff about residents' rights. Whenever you feel that one has been violated, the staff must be told and the practice changed. Have a copy of the Residents' Rights law in your possession so you can refer to it whenever you have a question. Refer to Chapter 2 for more information on residents' rights. That chapter does not include the entire text, so have your own copy on hand. The nursing home will have given your relative a personal copy at the time of admission. The social worker will give you one if you request it.

Some of the residents' rights infractions include not knocking on the residents' room doors, exposing the residents to public view on trips to and from the shower, discussing one resident in front of another, not offering choices, forcing medical treatment, withholding information, or monitoring communication.

Verbal, physical, and emotional abuse make follow-through mandatory. You will notice bruises and breaks, but also look at cleanliness and grooming. Residents should have good hair and mouth care, clean finger nails, eye glasses, and hearing aids, and no body odor. If your relative is confined to bed look for clean, dry bedding, understanding that it could have become wet just as you arrived. If you see bed sores report them immediately. Check for reddened areas, especially on heels, ankles, and buttocks. You can do this subtly by offering a back rub or applying lotion to your relative's skin. The nursing staff takes pride in keeping down the incidence of bed sores and will work hard to prevent and cure the decubitus ulcers.

Nursing home residents must be provided cold drinking water at their bedsides. Sometimes they do not drink it. They should have about ten glasses of liquid daily to prevent dehydration, which can lead to other problems evidenced by confusion and/or infections. Become suspicious of dehydration when you see very dry skin and mouth, sunken eyeballs, heavy speech, and unexplained drowsiness and confusion. Dehydration can occur rapidly. You can help prevent it by providing drinks during your visits. It is more palatable to take liquids as a treat with a friend than to drink because it is necessary.

Monitor to make sure your relative is addressed by the preferred name, treated respectfully and as an individual, and not labeled or called names. This is verbal and emotional abuse. Ignoring, mocking, poking fun, are unacceptable and illegal.

You may decide to talk to the administrator when you see problems that are beyond the staff's ability to address. Your relative may need some procedure or approach that no staff member can capably provide. If it is a service that should be offered in the nursing home, do some research and then present it to the administrator. You may also want the administrator to know if you think that the staff is obviously understaffed and overworked. If they cannot do what has to be done because of manpower limitations your relative will suffer. This problem will become apparent when there are falls, infections, wet and dirty residents, agitation, and increased use of physical and chemical restraints—results of the inability of the staff to give adequate attention and supervision.

Keep in mind that the administrator does not know everything that is going on. Through you the nursing home staff can be made aware of

1. which staff members are effective and which are a detriment;
2. the effectiveness and acceptability of the services delivered;
3. needs and problems of the resident and the family;
4. the public reaction to the nursing home program and staff;
5. trends and patterns, both good and grievous, in the nursing home's care.

HOW TO TALK WITH THE STAFF AND PROBLEM-SOLVE

It is not they against you or over you. Keep in mind that you and the staff have your relative's welfare foremost in mind. Also, see yourself and your relative as part of the care team. You cannot perform skilled procedures that take professional training and knowledge, but neither can all the staff do all things. Be egalitarian. You are all equal in the sense that it is a team approach. If your actions are based on this attitude the staff will want to work with you and your relative in a helpful, sustaining way.

If the staff feels you do not trust them, are looking for minute mistakes, and suggest that they do not know what they are doing, they will do what has to be done to placate you, but otherwise avoid you. Your reputation will be made and each employee will internally groan when you approach them, setting up a negative attitude before the first word leaves your mouth. Do not put yourself in that position. Although some individual staff members will be resistive no matter how diplomatic you are, most of the staff will appreciate and understand your concern if you also appreciate and understand what they have to say. Some techniques for talking with staff, keeping them on your side, and getting what you want while being assertive, follow.

1. Do not take what the other person says as a personal affront. People react to what is going on because of their own needs, not because of you. If they get defensive or accusing, remember that it is their problem and not because of what you have said.

For example:
If you ask whether or not the resident's water pitcher has been refilled today do not get into a confrontation if the nurse or nursing assistant counters with a retort stating that they are always filled everyday, or that there are other residents who need more attention, or they have other things to do. You did not cause the response, their own pressures did.

2. Do not meet anger with anger. In the last example, if you had responded defensively or in any way escalated the contact into an argument you would have compounded a single problem into an unhappy and unfortunate event. Continue matter-of-factly, and if necessary, explain that you are not accusing, but looking for assistance and information. Your goal is not to win a fight, but to get what you want. You can keep the control.

For example:
You can recognize that the staff is busy and responsible, but

the water pitcher appears to be empty and where can you go to get it filled?

3. Keep an even tone to your voice. People may forget what you said, but they will not forget how you said it.

Taking the water pitcher problem as a continuing example, your innocuous reply could be delivered with sarcasm, whining, or shouting. Then the acceptance and explanation would not have sounded like appeasement, but like denunciation. Your relationship with the staff would be set in the negative.

4. Role-play. In other words, rehearse. If you and your relative are having a problem and you want action, but not alienation, work out what you want to say, what message you want to give, and how you want to deliver it. Find someone to role-play with you. You can play your part and the other participant can play the nursing home staff member. Then reverse roles so you can simulate what it feels like to hear your complaint, concern, or request. Work out your most effective approach. Early groundwork that shows you to be a reasonable, but assertive, person will pay off in the future if and when more serious problems develop.

5. Know what you want. When you tell the staff of your dissatisfaction, give them some clue as to what would make you happy. If you want the water pitcher filled by 10:00 A.M. every day, state that. If time is negotiable, be ready to work out a reasonable time frame. If you will not dicker, be ready to explain why. Is your relative without water by that time? Does the resident always seem to get thirsty at 10:00 A.M.? Does he or she have to take medicine at that time, or need water when he or she has the midmorning snack?

6. Pick the person. Do not complain to the activity director about the laundry or to the nursing staff about the director of nursing. If you have a problem with your relative's roommate go to the person who works out room changes or can help work out the problem. This is the social worker.

Finding the appropriate person is one thing, finding a receptive person is another. If you can avoid it, do not deal with staff members who are unresponsive, irritable, and uncooperative.

For example:

If you can talk with any of the nurses about the water pitcher, pick the one who will listen and who can get things done.

7. Do not let problems pile up. There may be small irritations or little acts of neglect. You may decide these are not worth making a fuss about. Maybe, maybe not. What happens when you have a cluster of complaints, or see an ongoing pattern of corner cutting, is that you build up resentment that can explode when one more thing happens. The staff, not having been told of former problems, will not understand what seems to be an overreaction. You will get their attention, but not their active concern. Better that you bring occurrences to staff attention as they pop up. If you think they are small problems and that you might be quibbling over minutiae, say so, but at the same time let staff know you do not want your or your relative's concerns minimized. If little things can be worked out, everything seems easier.

8. Speak in the first person singular. Do not speak in the plural. Do not say "we think" or "we would like" unless that is really true. If you are talking on behalf of you and your relative or represent other residents and relatives "we" is appropriate. Otherwise, stand up for what you want by saying "I."

Also use the first person, I, when you are making your request or complaint rather than speaking about the person you are admonishing. Do not say you did this or you should do that. Say I want this or I want you to do this.

For example:

When Mrs. Z's daughter wanted to put a stop to unnecessary noise outside Mrs. Z's room she did not tell the staff they were too noisy and that they would have to do their chatting and giggling elsewhere. She said that she found the noise bothered her mother's concentration and made her suspicious. She said she would appreciate it if they could be quieter or talk elsewhere. The first example accuses. The second example explains.

9. Ask questions. If you do not know why something is done, ask. This is far better than jumping to conclusions and making yourself and everyone else unhappy. The staff have reasons for their actions and will explain them to you if you inquire in a way that indicates that you want to learn. Do not ask in a hostile, challenging way that turns people off and is frightening to the

staff. Many routine procedures are so automatic that staff do not think them through each time. Some of these may need to be looked at and revised. If you do not like the procedure and the reasons for it, you can take your concern to the administrator, who can do something about it.

10. Know your feelings. If you are unhappy about your relative's situation it will color your attitude about everything, particularly in regard to the nursing home. With this negative mindset everybody will have a hard time pleasing you. Try to realize that you feel bad because of circumstances and should not take out your despair on the staff. Instead, be honest and let them know how and why you are suffering. They will appreciate your frankness, understand because of their experience with others, and be supportive. However, if your discontent spills over into irritation toward them you will get no sympathy from them.

11. Let staff members know what you want. Staff members may err and tell you too much or too little. They cannot know your expectations unless you tell them what you want. Tell them when, what, and why. Better yet, put your information requirements in writing. Help the staff understand if you want a detailed, businesslike, or bottom-line report. And if it is impossible to reach you, give them a break and buy an answering machine.

12. Get the nursing assistants, and other staff, to visit your relative's room. Asking for more visits may get more in-room checking for your relative by nursing assistants. But it may be more effective to appeal to what they like to get them to stop by more often. The old standby is candy. Keep candies in a jar for staff. As they treat themselves they will interact with the resident. Post a joke, cartoon, or saying daily or weekly so the assistants will stop by to get the latest chuckle or bit of wisdom. Goodies and fun are an enticing combination. Use them to get things going the way you want them.

13. Always say, "Thank you." Let the staff know that they can please you by saying, "Thank you." Even if it is something that staff members do routinely or should have done earlier, say "Thank you." They will feel good about your thanks and will also feel good about you. They will know what to do the next time to curry your favor.

14. Ask. Do not demand. When you hear yourself saying, "You should," or "You must," stop yourself and make it a question. Say, "Will you," or, "Could you." You are saying the same thing, but in a much more acceptable way. People want to help. They do not want to obey orders.

15. Use humor. If you can see something from a humorous point of view, take advantage of that. People will be drawn to you and your needs if you can be casual and make it fun. This does not mean that you will make fun of people, but that you will laugh whenever you can and pick the funny elements out of situations.

16. See the staff's side. Recognize the staff members' responsibilities and pressures to do their duties. Realize that your request might seem like a small thing. State this. "I know you are busy, but———."

17. Ask the staff's opinion. If you have a problem, explain it and ask the staff if they have any suggestions for solving it or can recommend an approach. In this way they see that they can be of expert assistance and will try to work it out for you.

For example:

If your relative's food arrives cold, state the problem and ask if they can suggest a way to make an improvement.

18. Look pleasant. If you approach the staff members with a look of anger or disapproval they will immediately become apprehensive and expect the worst. If you look pleasant the staff member will be more receptive to what you have to say.

19. Apologize. If you complain, accuse, or become angry and you are wrong, acknowledge it and apologize. Even if you are right you can still apologize for losing your temper or making inappropriate comments. Do not apologize for your concerns and rightful complaints, only for actions that may have been detrimental.

20. Keep notes. Write down your concerns and observations. Note when and with whom you talk. Add what was done about the situation. Do not obviously maintain documentation because this makes the staff feel criticized and causes them to think that you are looking for problems. It is helpful, though, to be able to

know what you saw, when you saw it, when you reported it, and what was done. If results are not satisfactory you have accurate information to which you can refer.

21. Offer to help. Describe the problem and ask what you can do to make it better. Note the difficulty and suggest what you can do to help.
For example:
The food arrives cold. Ask if it would be helpful for you to go to the kitchen to pick it up.

22. Ask for a facilitator. When helpful communication is not taking place and problems are not being resolved, ask if an outside consultant can be obtained to facilitate discussion and resolution. Nursing homes have many consultants running in and out of the facility. The social work consultant might be a good choice as he or she is skilled in group work, relationship counseling, problem solving, and communication skills.

23. Request a meeting. The difficulty may be such that you want a quiet sit-down time for discussion and problem solving. Ask for a meeting with the appropriate person/s, stating what your topic will be. Make it clear why you want to talk with the person or people you have approached. If other staff members are there and you are not prepared to deal with a group, ask again for the meeting you wanted. If they refuse to comply with your request and you are not happy with the makeup of the group, leave and appeal to the person in the next higher level of authority.

24. Meet regularly. Ask to meet with key staff members weekly so you are guaranteed an ongoing dialogue. Meeting regularly will bring an adversary relationship into a partnership. Do not meet frivolously just for the sake of meeting. Meet if you feel there are unrecognized needs and if communication is difficult.
For example:
Ms AA wanted to guarantee her mother the very best. She felt that her relative was not getting the best of care in the nursing home. Since she knew what her mother needed she kept after various staff members to provide as she prescribed. She was invariably critical and demanding. Staff became snarly and de-

142 | The Nursing Home Experience

fensive and made every effort to avoid her. Their only hope was that Ms AA would move her mother to another facility. Since hope, avoidance, and nastiness did not solve the communication and care problem, they decided to meet together for one hour every month. Ms AA was full of complaints the first month, but she felt the staff heard her because they talked to her and she could see they were trying to give the required care. After two more meetings the problem seemed settled as everyone was more open and understanding. The meetings started a communication that could then be kept up without a formal get-together.

25. Attend inservice meetings. All nursing home staff members are required to attend yearly inservice meetings on communication with the impaired elderly, psychosocial needs of the elderly, and residents' rights, among others. As a basis for commonality, ask to attend these sessions so you will have a mutual background for discussion.

If all your efforts have failed even though you have been pleasant, reasonable, and assertive, other steps are required. You are your relative's advocate and in that role need to pursue the problem to a satisfactory conclusion.

As an advocate you want to address all problems as they arise, as well as give commendations and express appreciation for good care, programs, and people.

To be an advocate:

1. Seek out the facts. Try to look at all sides of the issue. Make sure your relative's complaints are based on real issues and not concerns related to general discontent that has little to do with the care provided and a lot to do with the relative's situation.

2. Discuss the problem with the appropriate staff member. Take nursing problems to the charge nurse, relationship problems and emotional concerns to the social worker, entertainment issues to the activity coordinator, food problems to the dietitian, laundry dissatisfactions to housekeeping, billing questions to accounting, and maintenance worries to maintenance. Allow time for investigation and change, but follow up if you do not get feedback within a few days.

3. If you are not satisfied with the results, go to the staff

person's supervisor, explaining why you are there. Do this up through the administrator, if necessary.

If resolution still eludes you, ask about the facility's grievance procedure and follow through with it. Be sure to document what you have done and who said what, when.

You may also want to talk with other family members and residents by way of the Family Council or the Resident Council to determine if there is widespread concern and others share your frustration.

If the problem is not addressed to your satisfaction after giving ample information and opportunity, move to influential sources outside the facility, such as:

a. Health Department. If unsafe health practices are involved report your concern to your local health department.

b. Long-term-care ombudsman. This telephone number is posted in the facility. That person investigates all complaints.

c. State Department of Health and Economic Services. Call the toll-free abuse hot line. The State Health and Economic Services Department staff will investigate within twenty-four hours if it is a matter of abuse.

d. State nursing home surveyors. The nursing home is inspected annually. Make it a point to talk with the survey team when they visit the facility, or call the State Licensure Department directly.

e. Home office. If the facility is part of a chain, call the home office to talk with the regional manager.

When all is said and done, remember:

1. You can put as much or as little as you need or want into being a part of what goes on in the nursing home.

2. You continue to be the vital link to your relative's past and to the community outside the facility, and are part of what gives the resident's life meaning.

3. How you handle yourself will, in large part, determine how the staff responds to you.

List of Communication Techniques

1. Do not take what the other person says as a personal affront
2. Do not meet anger with anger
3. Keep an even tone to your voice
4. Role-play
5. Know what you want
6. Pick the person
7. Do not let problems pile up
8. Speak in the first person singular
9. Ask questions
10. Know your feelings
11. Let staff members know what you want
12. Get the nursing assistants, and other staff, to visit your relative's room
13. Always say thank you
14. Ask. Do not demand
15. Use humor
16. See the staff's side
17. Ask the staff's opinion
18. Look pleasant
19. Apologize
20. Keep notes
21. Offer to help
22. Ask for a facilitator to help with communication
23. Request a meeting
24. Meet regularly
25. Attend inservice meetings

Glossary

ACTIVITIES OF DAILY LIVING Referred to as ADLs. Residents are described as independent or dependent in activities of daily living (ADL). They are independent if they can feed, dress, bathe, and toilet themselves. They are dependent if they need help in any of these areas of personal care.

ACTIVITY COORDINATOR Person in charge of the activity program in the nursing home. The coordinator is a department head and supervises other activity department employees and the volunteers.

ACTIVITY DEPARTMENT A separate department in nursing homes. The director reports to the administrator. The head of the department is responsible for devising an activity schedule for every resident in the facility, as well as providing therapeutic group experiences and programs.

ACTIVITY DIRECTOR See Activity Coordinator.

ADMINISTRATOR The chief executive officer of the nursing home. Administrators make the final decisions, address the most difficult problems, and are held responsible for the running of the facility. They are licensed by the state and are educated as health-care administrators.

ADMISSIONS The department that deals primarily with marketing, public relations, and admissions to the nursing home. Everyone inquiring about or entering a nursing home talks with and is guided by the admissions coordinator.

ADMISSIONS CONTRACT Spells out the resident's and the nursing home's responsibilities. It is variously known as the admissions agreement or the financial agreement.

146 | Glossary

ADMISSIONS COORDINATOR May head a separate department or be attached to social services or administration. Interprets the nursing home to the public, makes admission arrangements, and finalizes the necessary arrangements prior to admission.

ADULT PROTECTIVE SERVICES A part of the state health and economic services program. There is a toll-free telephone number to call at any time of the day or night to report to a centralized location any physical, emotional, or sexual abuse or exploitation. The central office assigns the report for investigation. An investigation must begin within twenty-four hours after the complaint was received and is usually conducted by social workers who make recommendations based on their findings.

ALZHEIMER'S DISEASE A degenerative brain disorder. Reasoning, memory, time, place, and person orientation are affected. It was first described by Dr. Alois Alzheimer in 1907. Symptoms appear gradually, with a decline in intellectual ability along with an accompanying physical decline that takes place over many years.

ANCILLARY STAFF All those on the staff who are not medically trained. This includes administration, social services, activities, food services, housekeeping, and maintenance staff.

ASSISTANT DIRECTOR OF NURSING Second in command after the director of nursing. This employee is a registered nurse, is licensed, and is cognizant of local, state, and federal nursing and nursing home rules and regulations.

ASSISTANT ADMINISTRATOR Assists the administrator and acts in the administrator's place in the administrator's absence. Sometimes assistant administrators are administrators in training.

BED SORES See Decubitus Ulcer.

CARE PLANS The plans of treatment. A care plan is prepared for each resident by the care team.

CARE TEAM All professionals employed in the facility; they are responsible for carrying out the plan of care. The care team is made up of the physician, nurse, physical, occupational, and speech therapists, social worker, dietitian, activities coordinator, and anyone else involved in working with the resident, such as a family member, a volunteer, a friend, a minister. Residents are to represent themselves on their own behalf as a care-team member.

CASE MANAGER An outside paid professional social worker who visits the nursing home and resident as requested by the resident or the resident's family. The case manager functions as a therapist, an advocate, a confidant, or an intermediary to arrange other services as needed.

CERTIFIED NURSING ASSISTANTS Have completed a course of training that qualifies them to provide personal care to medical patients.

CHARGE NURSE A registered nurse who is a graduate of a school of nursing and holds a license from the state. The charge nurse is in charge of a wing, floor, or area in the nursing home, is responsible for the assignment of duties, and supervises the certified nursing assistants.

CHEMICAL RESTRAINTS Medications given to residents who require sedation when they are disruptive. These are usually one or more of the minor or major tranquilizers.

COGNITIVE IMPAIRMENT A thinking disorder or problem wherein residents have difficulty with memory, interpretation, orientation, and judgment.

COMMUNICATION BOARD Ranges from a technologically sophisticated display to hand-made pictures, letters, and numbers. It assists residents who cannot speak by making it possible for them to spell out words or point to pictures to convey thoughts, needs, and desires.

CONFIDENTIALITY The law for all nursing home employees. They are not allowed to divulge any information regarding any resident to anyone without written consent, except in the case of medical care when the medical chart accompanies the resident to the medical appointment.

CONTRACTURES Caused by muscles shortening or contracting. Contractures are prevented by daily range of motion exercises.

CUSTODIAL CARE The care provided in a nursing home in the absence of a diagnosed medical problem that would require aggressive nursing care and medical procedures. The resident may need supervision and assistance, but no specialized nursing attention.

DECUBITUS ULCER An ulceration that is caused by prolonged pressure and usually found on bedridden residents.

DEPARTMENT HEAD Part of the administrative team of the nursing home and responsible for one part of the nursing home services. Some of the nursing home departments are social work, nursing, activities, food service, housekeeping, and physical services (maintenance).

DIRECTOR OF NURSING   Oversees the nursing department. A registered, licensed nurse responsible for nursing policies and procedures, job descriptions, hiring and firing, and resident safety and quality of care.

DISORIENTED   Nursing home residents can be disoriented, confused, unsure as to time, place, and person in any of those three areas, such as not to know what day it is, where they are, or who they are.

ELECTRONIC PROTECTION   Wrist or ankle bracelets worn by disoriented residents to protect them from dangerous wandering outside the nursing home. The electronic bracelets trigger an alarm when the residents attempt to exit the facility.

FAMILY COUNCIL   An organization made up of the family members of nursing home residents. It is sponsored by the nursing home, usually by the social service department. It is family-member governed and geared to family-member needs and interests.

GERICHAIR   A cumbersome, padded, vinyl covered chair that securely holds the resident in a sitting or semisitting position. It has wheels and can be pushed from place to place, but cannot be moved by the occupant of the chair.

HEAD NURSE   See Charge Nurse.

HEALTH AND REHABILITATIVE SERVICES   The state agency that encompasses most of the licensing, investigative, and payment agencies that govern nursing homes. The ombudsman, adult protective services, licensing and certification office, department of professional regulation, the health department, and Medicaid are all part of this state conglomerate.

HEALTH DEPARTMENT   Concerned with epidemics, contagion, and sanitation. It is authorized to investigate community health complaints, including nursing home irregularities.

HOME OFFICE   Some nursing homes are part of a chain and have home offices and tiers of administration. Regional or home offices are frequently located in states different from the location of the nursing home. Nevertheless, a chain of command is in charge of the facility. The nursing home administrator reports to the regional manager. Since chain nursing homes are generally run with universal policies and procedures for the group of facilities, you may decide to assist the local nursing home to adapt more to community needs.

Hoyer Lift A manually operated aid that moves the handicapped individual from one place to another, such as from chair to bed. The resident sits in a sling and the attendant runs the crank that lifts and moves the resident.

Intermediate Care A level of care in a nursing home that refers to the residents' need for supervision and assistance, but not for skilled medical procedures. The Medicaid payment for intermediate care is less than that for skilled care.

Licensed Practical Nurse Licensed practical nurses, or LPNs, are licensed by the state, have a degree in practical nursing, and are allowed to perform many skilled medical procedures such as administering medicines and providing treatments. They have fewer years of formal training than are required of a registered nurse.

Long-Term-Care Facility A nursing home that accepts residents for extended or continual care.

Long-Term-Care Ombudsman The ombudsman occupies a position required in each state as a result of the Older Americans' Act. The ombudsman is an advocate for nursing home residents and investigates all complaints on their behalf. The telephone number of the nearest ombudsman is posted in a public place in the nursing home for use by the residents and their families.

Marketing Nursing homes are frequently for-profit concerns and stay in business because they make money. To make money they must sell their product. Consequently, they market their services to keep their beds occupied to full capacity. Some nursing homes employ people to do their marketing, add it to other jobs such as admissions or social services, or rely on the home office to do the marketing.

Medicaid Administered by the state and available to nursing home residents who are eligible financially and medically. Those who need Medicaid payments to be able to enter and stay in a long-term-care facility are approved after application to and investigation by the state agency that administers the Medicaid program. Medicaid payments to nursing homes are lower than the facility's regular fee. As a consequence, residents who will be supported by Medicaid are less desirable to them than private pay residents. Once a Medicaid resident is accepted into a nursing home, the resident cannot be discharged to make room for a higher-paying resident unless the facility completely stops accepting all Medicaid funds.

MEDICAL CHART The resident's confidential chart that contains the medical history, diagnosis, course of treatment, and regular reports from all care-team departments. The chart is kept at the nursing station and available only to medical consultants, surveyors, investigators, and the resident, unless the resident gives written permission for others to examine it.

MEDICARE A federal insurance program for the disabled and those over age sixty-five, according to articles of the Social Security Act. Medicare pays for nursing home care for residents for a limited time for a limited number of rehabilitation and skilled medical procedures.

NURSING SUPERVISOR The level of supervision between the director of nursing and the charge nurse in the nursing home. The nursing supervisor is assigned various administrative and supervisory responsibilities.

OCCUPATIONAL THERAPIST Works with the residents to restore manual dexterity, eye-hand coordination, and adaptive skills, and works on improving activity of daily living abilities. Generally works part-time or serves as a consultant in the nursing home.

OMBUDSMAN See Long-Term-Care Ombudsman.

ORGANIC BRAIN SYNDROME Organic brain syndrome, OBS, refers to cognitive impairment problems such as memory loss, poor judgment, mistaken perceptions, disintegrating social functioning, and loss of self-care skills. Mental deterioration is accompanied by a slow physical deterioration.

PARKINSON'S DISEASE First described by James Parkinson in 1817. The cause is not known. It is a degenerative neurological disorder that results in trembling of the limbs, muscular stiffness, and slow body movement. Stooped posture, short, shuffling steps, and soft, rapid, mumbling speech are characteristic of the disease.

PATIENTS' RIGHTS See Residents' Rights.

POLICIES AND PROCEDURES Every nursing home has written policies and procedures that prescribe the way all departments and employees carry out their duties, based on the laws and the rules and regulations that govern nursing home operation. The nursing home staff cannot change the rules and regulations, but they can change their own policies and procedures as long as they continue to abide by the law.

Posey A physical restraint made of cloth. It is designed to keep residents from leaving their chairs or beds and wandering away or hurting themselves or others. The posey is attached to the resident and then tied to the chair or bed.

Physical Restraints Include the posey, gerichairs, bed rails, lap trays, and anything that prevents the residents from moving about at will. They are used to prevent falls, wandering away, and hurt to themselves or others.

Private-Pay Residents who pay the full cost for the nursing home out of their own funds.

Psychosocial The emotional, relationship, and activity needs of the nursing home residents.

Recreational Therapist A person who has a college degree in recreational therapy. This includes an understanding of using leisure skills to enhance growth in social, psychological, and physical areas.

Regional Manager Employed by a company that owns and/or manages a group of nursing homes. Oversees the nursing home operation and is the local nursing home administrator's boss.

Registered Nurse A registered nurse, RN, has a college degree in nursing and is licensed by the state. RNs give medications and provide skilled medical treatments following physicians' orders.

Rehabilitation Assistants Function under the supervision of a licensed physical therapist or nurse and perform ongoing restorative functions to aid the residents in maintaining strength, flexibility, and self-help skills.

Reminisce Reminiscing is used to help residents review their lives and find joy and fulfillment in their past.

Resident Council A self-governing body, made up of residents, that deals with all that concerns residents. It is set up to give residents a voice in the running of the nursing home. The officers of the group are residents. There is a staff adviser who is usually the activities coordinator.

Residents' Rights Residents' rights are guaranteed under federal law. Residents' Rights are a group of statements that assure nursing home residents of the same rights and responsibilities as those accorded any citizen of the United States. Each resident is given a copy of the Residents' Rights law when admitted to the nursing home.

RESTORATIVE NURSING The area of nursing that concentrates on helping residents maintain or improve in self-help and independence. Nursing homes generally have a separate restorative nursing department.

ROLE-PLAY Acting in the role of another in order to better understand that person's responses and reactions. Also used to rehearse a new role, such as when trying something one has not attempted previously, or when practicing to manage a difficult situation more effectively.

RULES AND REGULATIONS Written by state governmental agencies to interpret the pertinent laws so they may be put into action. They are enforced by employees of governing bodies. Nursing homes are directed by many rules and regulations. Their policies and procedures are based on rules and regulations.

SENILITY See Organic Brain Syndrome.

SHIFT Nursing homes offer around-the-clock medical supervision. This is provided by three shifts of nurses and nursing assistants. The usual shifts run for eight hours, from 7:00 A.M. to 3:00 P.M., 3:00 P.M. to 11:00 P.M., and 11:00 P.M. to 7:00 A.M.

SHORT-TERM MEMORY LOSS Seen in the early stages of progressive diseases that affect the function of the brain, such as Alzheimer's disease and organic brain syndrome. This means that the person forgets what happened today, but easily recalls what happened in the past. Long-term memory stays intact long after the short-term memory has failed.

SKILLED CARE Provided in skilled nursing facilities (SNF). They provide twenty-four-hour medical coverage under the supervision of a registered nurse and the direction of a physician, the medical director. Residents who require skilled care receive skilled nursing procedures or rehabilitation services.

SKIN BREAKDOWN See Decubitus Ulcer.

SOCIAL SERVICE DEPARTMENT The department devoted to administering to the psychosocial needs of the residents and their families.

SOCIAL WORK CONSULTANT A licensed social worker with a master's degree (MSW) who consults with the director of the social services department in the nursing home. This is required when the nursing home employee does not have the necessary social work education.

Social Worker   A department head in the social service department who works as a member of the care team and who addresses the emotional, social, behavioral, and material needs of the residents and their families.

Speech Therapist   Evaluates and provides assistance to all residents who will benefit from speech therapy, particularly those who have speech difficulties because of trauma to the brain, perhaps as in the case of a stroke or tumor patients.

Staff   All nursing home employees.

State Department of Health and Economic Services   See Health and Rehabilitative Services.

State Health and Welfare Department   See Health and Rehabilitative Services.

State Licensing and Certification Team   See State Licensure Department.

State Licensure Department   Each state has a licensure department that licenses various individuals, agencies, and institutions that provide skilled services to people. Nursing homes are surveyed yearly by the state licensure survey team to see if they are following the laws and the rules and regulations that govern nursing homes. Depending on what the survey team finds, they can close down the facility, put it on probation through provisional status, renew the nursing home's license to operate, or award it a superior rating. Nursing home staff work hard to achieve a superior rating because of the status and approval involved in the attribution and because the nursing home is then eligible for higher financial allowances from the state.

State Nursing Home Surveyors   See State Licensure Department.

Sundown Symptoms   Brain-injured residents, those with Alzheimer's disease, or those with organic brain syndrome may suffer agitation, paranoia, and confusion at night and may become severe management problems. Because these symptoms do not appear until after sundown they are called sundown symptoms.

Survey Team   See State Licensure Department.

TACTILE THERAPY   Used to stimulate the residents' sense of touch. The brain receives different messages as different textures are felt.

TEAM   See Care Team.

VETERANS ADMINISTRATION   The Veterans Administration can benefit nursing home residents who receive a disability pension from them. The VA will pay for their care in nursing homes that have agreed to accept VA payments and have signed an agreement with them.

WHEELCHAIR LIFT   Vehicles so equipped have a platform that lowers to accept the resident in the wheelchair and then raises the platform into the van. Vans that transport the elderly can be equipped with wheelchair lifts. Sometimes nursing homes own such vans. Frequently public service agencies in the community provide transportation services for wheelchair-bound residents.

Worksheet

I. When you are considering nursing home placement for a relative.

    A. Does the relative need more medical care than you can give?
       1. List medical problems.

_____

_____

_____

_____

_____

If there are more than four problems, or if one of them is Alzheimer's disease, stroke, Parkinson's disease, or organic brain syndrome, give yourself a point.

    B. Does the relative need more supervision than he or she is receiving?
       1. List supervision needs.

_____

_____

_____

_____

_____

If you list more than four, or if one is because he or she wanders away and gets lost, give yourself a point.

    C. Can you give the care needed?
       (Circle correct answer after each question)
        1. Do you have health problems?   Yes   No
          a. List your health problems.

        2. Do you have responsibilities for others?   Yes   No
          a. List the other people in your life and your obligations to them.

_____

_____

_____

_____

_____

        3. Do you work outside the home?   Yes   No
        4. Are you temperamentally unable to be a caregiver?   Yes   No
        5. Does the relative need more care than you can give?   Yes   No
        6. Do you and the relative have a strained relationship?   Yes   No
        7. Does your relative have feelings about being a burden to those he or she cares about?   Yes   No

Give yourself one point for each yes answer. If you have more than four points, seriously consider nursing home placement.

II. Where to place.

    A. Do you plan to visit your relative frequently?   Yes   No
       1. In that case, are there nursing homes near you?   Yes   No
       2. Is the local nursing home easy to get to?   Yes   No
    B. Does the nursing home look good?   Yes   No
       1. Does it appear to be clean?   Yes   No
       2. Does it smell clean?   Yes   No
       3. Is it well maintained?   Yes   No

4. Do you like the decor?   Yes   No
   5. Is the layout convenient and comfortable?   Yes   No
C. Do you feel good about the nursing home?   Yes   No
   1. Do the residents seem happy?   Yes   No
   2. Do you see interaction among staff and residents? Yes   No
   3. Do you like the staff members?   Yes   No
   4. Do the staff members appear to work well together? Yes   No
D. Licensing.
   1. Is the nursing home license provisional, regular, or superior?
   2. Is the administrator licensed?   Yes   No
E. Does the food look, smell, and taste good?   Yes   No
   1. Is it served attractively?   Yes   No
F. What activities does the facility provide that you think your relative will like?

_____

_____

_____

_____

_____

G. What does the facility charge?
   1. What are the additional charges?
   2. What amount is refunded if your relative does not stay an entire month?
   3. Does the facility hold the bed for the resident if the resident visits relatives or goes to the hospital?   Yes   No
   4. Does the nursing home accept Medicaid?   Yes   No
   5. Does the facility have a procedure for managing the residents' personal funds?   Yes   No
H. Special groups.
   1. Is there a resident council?   Yes   No
   2. Is there a family council?   Yes   No
   3. Are there other groups that meet in the facility, such as Alcoholics Anonymous, specialized groups for welcoming newcomers, groups for volunteers?   Yes   No
I. What kind of communication can you expect from the nursing home staff?
   1. Will staff notify you immediately of any changes?   Yes   No

Worksheet

    2. Will there always be someone available for you to talk with if you have questions or concerns? Yes No
    Who?
J. Will the staff help with discharge planning when your relative is ready to leave the nursing home? Yes No
    1. Which staff member is responsible for discharge planning?
    2. What resources can they arrange to assist your relative if continuing care is needed in the home?
K. What happens if your relative does not get along with a roommate?
    1. Are private rooms available?
L. Other special concerns, such as staffing, worship service availability, beauty salon, barber shop, transportation.

_____

_____

_____

_____

_____

III. Inventory of relative's belongings in the nursing home.
(Make this list and give a copy of it to the director of nursing and the social worker. Have a copy placed on the resident's medical chart. Keep it updated as possessions change or increase. Take an inventory about once every four months.)

A. Clothing items.
    1. Outer wear.

_____

_____

    2. Shoes.

_____

_____

3. Underwear.

___

___

4. Coats, sweaters.

___

___

5. Night wear.

___

___

6. Jewelry.

___

___

7. Accessories.

___

___

8. Miscellaneous.

___

___

___

B. Personal items.
   1. Decorative items.

___

___

Worksheet

　　2. Furniture.

　　3. Mementos.

　　4. Electronics.

　　5. Entertainment items.

　　6. Miscellaneous.

　C. Self-help items and health aids.
　　　1. Hearing aid.
　　　2. Glasses.
　　　3. Dentures.
　　　4. Walking aids.
　　　5. Wheelchair.
　　　6. Other.
　D. Grooming supplies.

IV. Nursing home adjustment.

   A. Attitude about placement.
      1. Did your relative agree to go to the facility? Yes   No
      2. Did he or she resist the move to the facility? Yes   No
      3. Did he or she insist he or she could continue to live in his/her own home (or yours)? Yes   No
   B. How did your relative deal with stress in the past?
      1. Good coping skills? Yes   No
      2. Slow, but steady adjustment? Yes   No
      3. Fell apart? Yes   No
   C. How many changes has your relative experienced over the past year?
      1. Health problems?

      2. Loss of home?

      3. Loss of independence?

      4. Financial setbacks?

      5. Loss of family members or friends?
   D. Is your relative a social or private person?
   E. Does your relative have interests or hobbies that can be maintained in the nursing home? Yes   No
   F. Has your relative had problems with anxiety or depression off and on throughout the years? Yes   No
   G. Does your relative have supportive friends and relatives? Yes   No
   H. Is your relative an optimist or a pessimist? The resident who accepts the necessity of nursing home placement, has good coping skills, has a positive outlook, has experienced minimal losses in the past year, and is a social person with interests, a stable personality, and supportive friends and relatives will make a good adjustment. The more the resident is the opposite of this profile, the more difficult the adjustment to the nursing home will be.

V. Handling problems in the nursing home.

   A. Identify the problem.
   B. Determine if the problem is caused by your relative, a staff member, a nursing home policy, or by your own distress.
   C. Pick the appropriate person to see about the problem.
      1. If it is your relative's problem, see the social worker.
      2. If it is a problem caused by a staff member, talk with the staff member. If necessary, move up the hierarchy to the administrator and then to the ombudsman.
      3. If the problem is caused by a nursing home policy, go to the administrator.
      4. If the problem is your own personal adjustment and distress, see the social worker.
   D. Keep dated notes on the problem, with whom you talked, what was said, what was done.
   E. Follow up to see the problem through to solution and to thank those that helped solve the problem.
   F. Assist your relative's adjustment.
      1. What does your relative need?
         a. Social skills? Yes No
         b. Hobbies and interests? Yes No
         c. Help for pain? Yes No
         d. Hope? Yes No
         e. Rehabilitation therapy? Yes No
         f. Help for emotional problems? Yes No
         g. A way to deal with anger or anxiety? Yes No
         h. Friends? Yes No
         i. Meaningful activity? Yes No
         j. Belonging? Yes No
         k. Attention? Yes No
         l. A change of room or roommate? Yes No
         m. Other?
      2. Follow the handling-problems process. Make notes. Try to see if there is a pattern.

VI. Visiting in the nursing home.

   A. Visits will be how often and when?
   B. Unsuccessful visits occurred on which dates? What were the content and activity of these visits?

_____

_____

_____

C. Keep notes on successful visits.

_____

_____

_____

_____

THE CROSSROAD COUNSELING LIBRARY
Books of Related Interest

James Archer, Jr.
COUNSELING COLLEGE STUDENTS
A Practical Guide for Teachers, Parents, and Counselors
"Must reading for everyone on campus—professors, administrators, dorm personnel, chaplains, and friends—as well as parents and other counselors to whom college students turn for support."—*Dr. William Van Ornum* $17.95

Denyse Beaudet
ENCOUNTERING THE MONSTER
Pathways in Children's Dreams
Based on original empirical research, and with recourse to the works of Jung, Neumann, Eliade, Marie-Louise Franz, and others, this book offers proven methods of approaching and understanding the dream life of children. $17.95

Robert W. Buckingham
CARE OF THE DYING CHILD
A Practical Guide for Those Who Help Others
"Buckingham's book delivers a powerful, poignant message deserving a wide readership."—*Library Journal* $17.95

Alastair V. Campbell, ed.
A DICTIONARY OF PASTORAL CARE
Provides information on the essentials of counseling and the kinds of problems encountered in pastoral practice. The approach is interdenominational and interdisciplinary. Contains over 300 entries by 185 authors in the fields of theology, philosophy, psychology, and sociology as well as from the theoretical background of psychotherapy and counseling. $24.50

David A. Crenshaw
BEREAVEMENT
Counseling the Grieving throughout the Life Cycle
Grief is examined from a life cycle perspective, infancy to old age. Special losses and practical strategies for frontline caregivers highlight this comprehensive guidebook.
$17.95 hardcover $10.95 paperback

Paul J. Curtin
HIDDEN RICHES
Stories of ACOAs on the Journey of Recovery
A book of hope and healing for every ACOA or for anyone who knows and loves someone who grew up in a dysfunctional family. $8.95 paperback

Paul J. Curtin
TUMBLEWEEDS
A Therapist's Guide to Treatment of ACOAs
A book for those who are ACOAs and for those who wish to help ACOAs in their search to experience and share themselves honestly. $7.95 paperback

Paul J. Curtin
RESISTANCE AND RECOVERY
For Adult Children of Alcoholics
The ideal companion to *Tumbleweeds, Resistance and Recovery* shows how resistance is vital and necessary to recovery when obstacles are turned into growth opportunities.
$7.95 paperback

Reuben Fine
THE HISTORY OF PSYCHOANALYSIS
New Expanded Edition
"Objective, comprehensive, and readable. A rare work. Highly recommended, whether as an introduction to the field or as a fresh overview to those already familiar with it."
—*Contemporary Psychology* $24.95 paperback

Paul G. Quinnett
SUICIDE: THE FOREVER DECISION
*For Those Thinking About Suicide,
and For Those Who Know, Love, or Counsel Them*
New Expanded Edition
"A treasure— this book can help save lives."—*William Van Ornum, psychotherapist and author* $9.95 paperback

Paul G. Quinnett
WHEN SELF-HELP FAILS
A Guide to Counseling Services
A guide to professional therapy. "Without a doubt one of the most honest, reassuring, nonpaternalistic, and useful self-help books ever to appear."—*Booklist* $11.95

Judah L. Ronch
ALZHEIMER'S DISEASE
A Practical Guide for Families and Other Caregivers
Must reading for everyone who must deal with the effects of this tragic disease on a daily basis. Filled with examples as well as facts, this book provides insights into dealing with one's feelings as well as with such practical advice as how to choose long-term care. $11.95 paperback

Theodore Isaac Rubin, M. D.
ANTI-SEMITISM: A Disease of the Mind
"A most poignant and lucid psychological examination of a severe emotional disease. Dr. Rubin offers hope and understanding to the victim and to the bigot. A splendid job!"—*Dr. Herbert S. Strean* $14.95

Theodore Isaac Rubin, M.D.
CHILD POTENTIAL
Fulfilling Your Child's Intellectual, Emotional, and Creative Promise
Information, guidance, and wisdom—a treasury of fresh ideas for parents to help their children become their best selves.
$18.95 hardcover $11.95 paperback

John R. Shack
COUPLES COUNSELING
A Practical Guide for Those Who Help Others
An essential guide to dealing with the 20 percent of all counseling situations that involve the relationship of two people. $17.95

Herbert S. Strean as told to Lucy Freeman
BEHIND THE COUCH
Revelations of a Psychoanalyst
"An entertaining account of an analyst's thoughts and feelings during the course of therapy."—*Psychology Today*
$11.95 paperback

Stuart Sutherland
THE INTERNATIONAL DICTIONARY OF PSYCHOLOGY
This new dictionary of psychology also covers a wide range of related disciplines, from anthropology to sociology. $49.95

Joan Leslie Taylor
IN THE LIGHT OF DYING
The Journals of a Hospice Volunteer
"Beautifully recounts the healing (our own) that results from service to others, and might well be considered as required reading for hospice volunteers." —Stephen Levine, author of *Who Dies?* $17.95

Montague Ullman, M.D. and Claire Limmer, M.S., eds.
THE VARIETY OF DREAM EXPERIENCE
Expanding Our Ways of Working With Dreams
"Lucidly describes the beneficial impact dream analysis can have in diverse fields and in society as a whole."—*Booklist*
$19.95 hardcover $14.95 paperback

William Van Ornum and Mary W. Van Ornum
TALKING TO CHILDREN ABOUT NUCLEAR WAR
"A wise book. A needed book. An urgent book."
—*Dr. Karl A. Menninger*
$15.95 hardcover $7.95 paperback

Kathleen Zraly and David Swift, M. D.
ANOREXIA, BULIMIA, AND COMPULSIVE OVEREATING
A Practical Guide for Counselors and Families
New and helpful approaches for everyone who knows, loves, or counsels victims of anorexia, bulimia, and chronic overeating. $17.95

At your bookstore, or to order directly, call 1-800-937-5557 or send your check or money order (adding $2.50 extra per book for postage and handling, up to $10.00 maximum) to: The Crossroad Publishing Company, 370 Lexington Avenue, New York, NY, 10017. Prices are subject to change.